Mentoring Teachers in Post-Compulsory Education

The post-compulsory sector is complex and multifaceted, with highly diverse and sometimes challenging learner groups and subject to change from almost unending shifts in educational policy. Effective mentoring has a crucial role in the initial training of new teachers in the post-compulsory sector offering them the guidance and practical support they need to respond to these challenges.

Now in its second edition, *Mentoring Teachers in Post-Compulsory Education* has been updated with current research and technological advances. Describing all of the expectations, responsibilities and rewards involved in mentoring, the book covers:

- what to expect as a mentor and what your trainee expects of you
- the skills, attributes and functions that make an effective mentor
- organising and conducting observations
- perspectives on professional learning
- what to do when things go wrong.

Accessible, practical and supportive, this book will help make mentoring an easier, more enjoyable and rewarding experience for all new mentors in the post-compulsory sector.

Bryan Cunningham is Senior Lecturer in Education, and Director of Quality Assurance, Faculty of Policy and Society at the Institute of Education, University of London.

Mentoring Teachers in Post-Compulsory Education

A guide to effective practice

Second edition

Bryan Cunningham

Routledge
Taylor & Francis Group

LONDON AND NEW YORK

First edition published 2005
by David Fulton Publishers

11 JAN 2012

11|12

This second edition published 2012
by Routledge
2 Park Square, Milton Park, Abingdon, Oxon OX14 4RN

Simultaneously published in the USA and Canada
by Routledge
711 Third Avenue, New York, NY 10017

Routledge is an imprint of the Taylor & Francis Group, an informa business

British Library Cataloguing in Publication Data
A catalogue record for this book is available from the British Library

Library of Congress Cataloging in Publication Data
Cunningham, Bryan, 1951- Mentoring teachers in post compulsory education : a guide to effective practice / Bryan Cunningham. — 2nd ed.
    p. cm.
Includes index.
1. Mentoring in education–Great Britain. 2. Teachers–In-service training–Great Britain. 3. Post-compulsory education–Great Britain. I. Title.
LB1731.4.C86 2012
371.1020941—dc23
                                        2011020085

ISBN: 978-0-415-66939-9 (hbk)
ISBN: 978-0-415-66940-5 (pbk)
ISBN: 978-0-203-81595-3 (ebk)

Typeset in Aldine
by HWA Text and Data Management, London

MIX
Paper from
responsible sources
FSC® C004839
www.fsc.org

Printed and bound in Great Britain by
CPI Antony Rowe, Chippenham, Wiltshire

Contents

Illustrations

Figures

Tables

Foreword

Lorna Unwin

Educational institutions tend not to see themselves as workplaces. Their focus is on the learning of their students (broadly defined) and, hence, considerations about how the workplace of the school, college or university might be organised in such a way as to maximise the learning potential of staff tend to be given very little attention. These institutions will probably have some form of 'staff development' programme or, in the bigger ones, even a staff development unit, but the approach tends to be one of offering 'courses' or workshops on specific themes (e.g. *using technology in learning*, or *improving time management*). Attending a 'course' is seen as the way to learn and so staff development mirrors the core activity of the institution – students learn through attending courses and so do staff. This is very curious given the considerable influence over the past thirty or so years of social theories of learning on education and training, and on workforce development. Using metaphors such as 'learning as participation' and 'learning as co-configuration', these theories explain how the most effective learning often occurs through active participation with others in solving problems, creating new artefacts and ideas, and, importantly, sharing knowledge and experience in a mutually supportive environment.

Social theories of learning are being used to help transform workplaces and the way work is organised. Learning happens in all workplaces, regardless of the type of work and the conditions in which it takes place. Yet, too often, this learning is under-utilised or, at worst, not recognised and rejected. For some employees, learning at work is restricted to learning how to survive or how to 'get around' inefficient management systems. There is a considerable body of research evidence that shows how those organisations that involve their employees in decision-making and afford them the discretion to make judgements without having to constantly get the approval of superiors are likely to be more productive, have lower levels of staff turnover, and are more likely to be sustainable (see Felstead *et al.*, 2009). When employees are trusted and their expertise valued, the workplace will be fulfilling its potential as a learning environment.

One of the key features of what Alison Fuller and I have called an 'expansive learning environment' is a robust framework of support for those who are developing their expertise (Fuller and Unwin, 2010). This applies to young people on apprenticeships or traineeships, to newcomers to an organisation, and to individuals who are changing and/or developing their roles. Mentoring forms a vital component of such a framework. In the case of trainee teachers in the post-compulsory education and training (PCET) field, it is through the support of a mentor that they will gain access to the wealth of expertise in their organisation and beyond. In their seminal work on 'situated learning', Jean Lave and Etienne Wenger introduced the concept of 'communities of practice'. They argued that a 'novice' entering the community has the status of a 'legitimate peripheral participant', which means that they have the right to be involved in the full life of the community and to learn from their more expert colleagues who, in turn, must make their knowledge and skills transparent and share them with the novice. In that way, the community can reproduce. Some commentators have pointed to the potentially conservative nature of Lave and Wenger's (1991) ideas, arguing that the novice is expected to adapt to the community rather than to challenge its ways of working (Hughes *et al.*, 2007. However, Lave and Wenger's theory remains influential because it describes how learning occurs in workplaces in a way that most people find instantly recognisable. When the supportive framework is in place and learning is seen as central to the life of the community, then people flourish.

In this book, Bryan Cunningham provides a detailed account of the concept and process of mentoring in the PCET context. The book should be read by everyone involved in and responsible for workforce development in colleges and other PCET-related organisations for it presents the tools to construct a framework of support to sustain communities of practice within institutions. Bryan traces the development of the mentoring concept as part of professional formation and development and draws attention to the challenges that mentors face, particularly in the dynamic world of PCET. As he rightly points out, mentors also need mentors.

References

Felstead, A., Fuller, A., Jewson, N., and Unwin, L. (2009) *Improving Working for Learning*, London: Routledge.

Fuller, A., and Unwin, L. (2010) Workplace Learning and the Organisation, in Malloch, M., Cairns, L., Evans, K., and O'Connor, B. N. (eds), *The SAGE Handbook of Workplace Learning*, London: SAGE.

Hughes, J., Jewson, N., and Unwin, L. (2007) (eds) *Communities of Practice: Critical Perspectives*, London: Routledge.

Lave, J., and Wenger, E. (1991) *Situated Learning*, Cambridge: Cambridge University Press.

Lorna Unwin is Professor of Vocational Education and Deputy Director of the ESRC-funded LLAKES Research Centre at the Institute of Education, University of London. After working as a journalist, she became interested in education whilst acting as a volunteer adult literacy tutor at university. She then taught in further education colleges and adult community education, and worked as an Education Officer for a large retail chain in the UK. She has held academic posts at the Open University and University of Sheffield. From 2003 to 2006, she was Director of the Centre for Labour Market Studies at the University of Leicester. Her book, *Teaching and Learning in Further Education* (co-authored with Prue Huddleston) is published by Routledge.

Introduction to the second edition

Since the publication of this guide in 2005 a number of highly important changes have taken place in the post-compulsory landscape that appear to warrant an updating and extension of the original book. Furthermore, from the perspective of how it has been evaluated (at least in so far as has been illustrated by the kinds of written or verbal feedback I have received) a second edition of *Mentoring Teachers in Post-Compulsory Education* stood to benefit from certain small – but significant – refinements that were being suggested. I also viewed the opportunity offered by a second edition as one that would allow me, for example, to incorporate a rather fuller range of theoretical perspectives on mentoring, and on the organisational 'architectures' that seem to best support the activity.

Without aiming to offer a *comprehensive* overview of the changes we have witnessed over the past seven years, I endeavour to outline below some of those that actually or potentially have the largest impact on the lives of teachers in the post-compulsory sector. (I have not attempted to deal with mapping the various significant changes to the organisation and funding of the PCET sector, given that these appear to be ongoing). As will become evident, a number of the developments to which I draw attention are in fact not ones that are exclusive to this sector of education: we can discern some shifts in policy or practice as having equal, if not even greater, relevance to our practitioner colleagues in both the school and higher education sectors. It is also probably useful to note that sometimes a change has not meant something akin to the dawning of a new era, but simply a marked accentuation of a trend already starting to be noticed when the first edition of the book was published. This observation applies, for instance, to the increasingly fuzzy dividing line between 'compulsory' and 'post-compulsory' sites of learning.

Broadly speaking, it seems possible to group recent major changes under five headings:

- Changes in policy and 'principles'
- Developments in pedagogy
- The evolving nature of learner groups
- The extension of the roles and responsibilities of classroom practitioners
- The further enhancement of the status and role of mentoring – often as a result of changes in the above four domains.

These are, at any rate, those I will be referring to at relevant points in this new edition. Each therefore seems to warrant a relatively brief commentary, and some illustration, which I now provide.

Changes in policy and 'principles'

These can perhaps most productively be considered as either national or local (i.e. organisational) changes. Occasionally, as will be evident from certain of the examples that follow, changes will of course need to be described as both national and local ones.

A significant change linking both policy and principles is the move to bring about a situation in which the majority of the teaching workforce is qualified to master's degree level; the notion of an 'all-graduate' profession is now being superseded by such a shift. It accords with developments in the school sector, which has seen the introduction of a Master's in Teaching and Learning (MTL) qualification. In a number of the UK's more selective sixth form colleges, M-level qualifications are even now held by many applicants for posts in them; further afield, in US community colleges higher degrees – often including doctorates – are already virtually the norm. Although from some perspectives it might seem that in such a context as a general further education college requiring M-level degrees is an unwarranted 'qualification escalation' or 'inflation', for many reasons it represents a logical step towards the goal of achieving for PCET teachers a less easily contested professional status. Furthermore, if we are to see an expansion of the 'HE in FE' trend, with more universities seeking arrangements with colleges to allow the latter to offer their degree-level programmes (and some colleges even seeking their own degree-awarding powers), then in fact we can see that holding a higher degree may be both appropriate and necessary.

A further significant potential development arises from one of the interesting recommendations of the Wolf Review of Vocational Education (Wolf, 2011). This relates to the fact that although at the time of writing teachers training to teach in the post-compulsory sector work towards QTLS (Qualified Teacher, Learning and Skills[1]) this qualification lacks parity with the far longer established QTS (Qualified Teacher Status) held by teachers who have successfully completed their training to teach in state schools. At present secondary-trained teachers may, if they wish, move to posts in, say, FE colleges, but the reverse does not hold true. Wolf proposes that QTLS be deemed as having complete parity with QTS, facilitating the removal of what from some perspectives has become a rather anomalous situation; if schools are to offer a broader range of skills-based qualifications, then they would potentially have access to a larger pool of professionals with expertise in working with young people on vocational pathways. One implication of the policy change, if it were approved, would seem to be that initial teacher training for PCET could become more attractive, because the qualification currently on offer, QTLS, then presents itself as having even greater 'transportability'. In such an environment it therefore seems likely that training programmes could increase in size, and paralleling such a development the number of mentors required could expand.

Nationally, of course, another major policy development arises from the demise in 2005 of the Further Education National Training Organisation (FENTO) and its replacement by the linked bodies Lifelong Learning UK (LLUK) and Standards Verification UK (SVUK). However, although the first edition of this book made a number of links between the realities of teachers' and mentors' work and the requirements to demonstrate awareness of, and compliance with, FENTO 'Standards', I have chosen not to follow a similar approach in this new edition. I feel it would be unwise to do so, given the highly uncertain position of many governmental and non-governmental bodies at the time of writing. I would further justify my decision by claiming that LLUK/SVUK's[2] conceptions of effective professional practice hardly differed radically from those of FENTO – and in turn will quite probably be mirrored by any that are set out by a possible new body with an interest in, or jurisdiction over, the practice of PCET teachers. However, for readers interested in a detailed breakdown of the overarching standards as specified *at the time of writing*, these can be found at: http://www.lluk.org/documents/standards/professional standards for itts 020107.pdf

Locally, the imperatives causing PCET institutions to be more or less constantly self-assessing the quality of the learning experiences they are providing, monitoring the impact of these, demonstrating that they are – even when generally held to be 'effective' – actively trying to enhance quality rather than being complacent, or 'coasting', are all ones that ultimately practitioners bear the brunt of. Preparing new teachers to deal with the procedures (and proformas!) entailed in such matters as regular internal audits, peer reviews of classroom practice and so on is now an essential component of mentors' roles; it may in fact also be one that they find themselves involved in even where more experienced teachers are struggling to adapt to increasingly stringent regimes of auditing, appraisal and inspection.

The quality of the learning that is being provided by higher education institutions (HEIs) has also been subject to increasingly rigorous scrutiny, not least of course by students themselves, given the greater financial burdens many are experiencing, principally as a result of higher course fees. Students also have understandably raised anxieties in recessionary times concerning whether the qualifications they are working towards will help them find eventual employment. From the point of view of how HEIs' provision of initial teacher training is judged – not only for PCET but for all sectors – the OfSTED inspection regime is especially important, and in particular the way in which the grade awarded for the quality of an HEI's training programme is relatively strongly influenced by the appropriateness and effectiveness of its associated mentoring framework. The OfSTED view is that it is *subject-specific* mentoring that is of paramount significance – hence the major efforts made by HEIs to secure assurances from their partner institutions that such subject-specificity will be on offer to trainees. For mentors, the major implication of the increased significance being attached to subject specialism is that they will need to ensure they are as up to date as possible with developments in their field, not only in terms of content knowledge but also with regard to pedagogic innovations that extend the repertoire of best practice in the teaching of the subject.

Developments in pedagogy

There have been really quite profound developments in this area, ones almost too extensive to list. We have seen far greater emphasis being given to the merits of differentiation in classrooms, with an extension of the notion to the rather broader one of *personalised learning*. This brings with it greater challenges, especially for relatively inexperienced teachers, in particular in settings where large learner groups are now the norm.

Classroom technologies have rapidly moved on from being largely dependent on the kinds of aids to learning referred to in the first edition of this book, with expectations now being placed on both teachers and learners that they will make extensive use of such technologies; the high standards of design and production of our learning materials that are now possible mean that using anything less than professional-looking aids in our classrooms has become out of the ordinary.

The above observation relates strongly to one particular overarching, and inescapable, trend that has accelerated enormously even during the lifespan of the first edition of this book; this is of course the use of information and communications technology, especially among the young. The 'Web 2.0 Generation' is adept at exploiting mobile technologies not only as the medium – perhaps the principal medium – for their social networking, but increasingly for educational purposes. Teachers who find it hard to adapt to these realities (and almost certainly some more mature teachers will find themselves in this position) are at risk of being dubbed dinosaurs – or on the wrong side of a dividing line between themselves as 'digital immigrants', with their learners, the 'digital natives', on the other.

Recently the environmental responsibility and sustainability agendas have become much more prominent within learning and teaching contexts, as they have more broadly in society. Such matters do impact on practitioners: it would be a somewhat out-of-touch mentor who did not caution a new teacher regarding the need to be aware of the environmental costs of over-generously supplying learners with 'one-use only' printed or other learning materials, for example. If mentors don't raise this sort of issue, it may well be that more environmentally minded learners will.

The evolving nature of learner groups

In the first edition of this book I drew attention to the incredible diversity of learners that come to the post-compulsory sector. This diversity has increased yet further, for a variety of reasons. One element of increasing diversity has been the *de facto* raising of the age up to which it is expected that the great majority of young people will remain in full-time education or training; in reality a present official 'leaving age' is now shading from 17 into 18. We hear the rather depressing term 'NEETS'[3] for those young people who are not yet demonstrating either their ability or their propensity to 'stay on', or to find gainful employment. This brings with it further – although by no means brand-new – challenges for teachers in the sector, challenges arising perhaps from the kind of poor motivation experienced by some young people when they perceive they are remaining in education only as a last resort.

Other 'cohort' matters impacting on teachers include the arrival, especially in some inner-city areas, of new migrant groups either fleeing the chaotic conditions of 'failed states' or taking advantage of the removal of barriers to movement within the much-expanded European Union. Increasing numbers of our younger learners (as young as 14 in some cases) are in post-compulsory education as an alternative to 'schooling' where the latter has either rejected them, or they have rejected it. These kinds of trends call for teachers to build their professional resilience, extend their pedagogic repertoire and engage yet more fully with notions of *nurturing* – prime examples of the kinds of areas in which the support and guidance of a skilled mentor can make a crucial difference.

Ironically, however, despite the depiction under the previous subheading of what is now an almost universal take-up of personal ICT among the young, it is at the same time probably true to say that the incidence of real disadvantage among our learners has also increased. Rising unemployment in recessionary times may mean that many of our younger learners come to us from homes where there is no wage-earner; family breakdown can mean that many of these homes will also be single-parent households. The furore over the withdrawal of Education Maintenance Allowances (EMAs), and their replacement by – less generous – bursaries seems indicative of the real anxieties being experienced by families in connection with the expense of continuing in full-time study.

In such circumstances the need for post-compulsory institutions to offer a secure and nurturing environment seems fairly self-evident. There are benefits to practitioners of becoming more aware of the ways in which inter-agency working takes place (for example involving possible liaison with the police or social work departments); knowing how to access, or make referral to, such other professionals can make literal life or death differences. Although issues of child protection remain of more importance in school settings, the PCET sector has also certainly had to engage with the 'Every Child Matters' (2004) agenda, and with *safeguarding* in particular, and take on board the need for even greater care in its recruitment processes (HMG, 2006).

The extension of the roles and responsibilities of classroom practitioners

In some senses, teachers in PCET have been beleaguered by curricular and organisational changes. They have of necessity had to become what Eric Hoyle long ago termed *extended* (as contrasted with *restricted*) professionals (Hoyle, 1974). Viewed from a positive perspective, one form of extension might well be engagement with mentoring as a dimension of their professional work. However, in a number of ways the 'flexibility' which teachers have been called upon to display is almost certainly experienced by busy teachers as to varying degrees unwelcome.

One commentator has viewed the PCET sector as one that has been 'running ever faster down the wrong road' (Coffield, 2007), by which was meant the apparently constant search for panaceas in the form of new curricular initiatives. A slightly earlier perspective was contained in an important OfSTED report, which drew attention to the fact that some of our less successful colleges appeared to suffer from a lack of clarity over their mission (OfSTED, 2004) – possibly, in my own view, because endless change has led to disorientation and confusion in some quarters over such matters as what exactly an institution's mission should be. In such circumstances, it seems small wonder that the needs for mentoring support expressed by many new classroom teachers have been accentuated.

In a number of ways, the responsibilities of PCET teachers have formally been added to yet further over recent years. It is now highly unusual for *full-time* posts to be advertised without them including explicit references to the need for successful applicants to assume functions in the realms of programme and team management, curriculum design, marketing and outreach, pastoral work and – increasingly often – coaching others. Each of these disparate activities carries its own set of obligations, and its own necessities for networking, self-organisation and even sometimes skills in the area of insider research, or action research. They have their own *discourse*, too, leaving us in sum with a situation where teachers must contend with, and respond constructively to, multiple discourses (Barnett, 2008: 200).

These are all sectoral issues that will tax new teachers – and often those more experienced, as well – and only add to the likelihood of mentoring being able to fulfil a highly worthwhile role in supporting such teachers. The centrality of mentors' work in aiding teachers' professional formation, and their professional resilience, is in my view now irrefutable.

The further enhancement of the status and role of mentoring

Mentoring has grown phenomenally in importance. It is being used increasingly in such contexts as social inclusion (Colley, 2003, Colley *et al.*, 2007), the advancement of black and minority ethnic (BME) groups, work with ex-offenders and – in a vastly contrasting sphere to this last – as a strategy for supporting some of the highest achieving individuals in business and in education to rise to the very top of their fields. New headteachers, for instance, are mentored by experienced and successful heads so that the professional performance of the former group is enhanced yet further, and so that, e.g., they are able to seek advice on improvement strategies they are contemplating introducing into their schools (Luck, 2003).

One spin-off of the situation involving the extremely widespread use of ICT, described above, has been the sad – in some cases tragic – rise of 'cyberbullying', the persecution and harassment by mobile phone of young people by their peers. The victims of such cruel behaviour (and of other, more traditional, forms of bullying) now, however, have access to 'cybermentors' – a kind of 'Samaritans Plus' service, staffed by volunteer youngsters who have themselves been victimised in similar ways (For an interesting flavour of the work of cybermentors – a project under the auspices of the funded charity Beatbully's work – see http://cybermentors.org.uk.)

Such examples as those above are many and varied – far too many, in fact, to cite in this brief introduction. The cumulative effect of what we have been witnessing is in my view the very significant embedding in the public consciousness of mentoring as a process of central, rather than in any way marginal, importance in supporting those in need of support. In academia we have, paralleling this expanded consciousness, a lengthening list of formal mentoring-related qualifications that individuals can work towards – up to and including a professional doctorate[4] – that will both extend their mentoring skills and assist in their career development.

Certain of the themes and trends reviewed under these five subheadings will be returned to in the relevant chapters of this new edition; some will be further explored more fully than others. In many ways, however, the original contents of *Mentoring Teachers in Post-Compulsory Education* have, I hope, stood the test of time. The principles and practices of effective mentoring that I outlined in 2005 are ones I believe are still current, valid and purposeful – and they are ones on which I continue to base my own professional work with colleagues in need of support and guidance.

Acknowledgement

I am very grateful to Michael Pinnock, whose insightful comments on my review of recent changes impacting on the PCET sector were invaluable.

References

Barnett, R. (2008) Critical professionalism in an age of supercomplexity, in B. Cunningham (ed.), *Exploring Professionalism,* London: Institute of Education, University of London.

Coffield, F. (2007) *Running Ever Faster down the Wrong Road: An Alternative Future for Learning and Skills,* London: Institute of Education, University of London.

Colley, H. (2003) *Mentoring for Social Inclusion: A Critical Approach to Nurturing Mentoring Relationships,* London and New York: Routledge Falmer.

Colley, H., Boetzelen, P., Hoskins, B., and Parveva, T. (2007) (eds) *Social Inclusion for Young People: Breaking Down the Barriers,* Strasbourg: Council of Europe.

Department for Education and Skills (2004) *Every Child Matters* (Green Paper), London: DfES.

Her Majesty's Government (2006) *Working Together to Safeguard Children: A Guide to Inter-Agency Working to Safeguard and Promote the Welfare of Children,* London: HMG.

Hoyle, E. (1974) Professionality, professionalism and control in teaching, *London Educational Review,* 3/2: 13–19.

Luck, C. (2003) *It's Good to Talk: An Enquiry into the Value of Mentoring as an Aspect of Professional Development for New Headteachers,* Nottingham: National College for School Leadership.

OfSTED (2004) *Why Colleges Fail,* Research Report HMI 2408, London: OfSTED.

Wolf, A. (2011) *Review of Vocational Education* (The Wolf Report), London: Department for Education.

Mentoring in context

Chapter objectives

- to situate mentoring within a broader context
- to provide some perspectives on an appropriate 'architecture' for the activity.

> Mr Tollmun-Jones would despise anything I am associated with, because he can't stand me. I can't blame him; I'd loathe me if I had to try teaching me algebra – but I would start by telling me what the point of it is. He never has and I'm not very enthusiastic about pointless subjects.
>
> (Christopher Metcalfe, public schoolboy, in Corlett, 1995)

Introduction

When a little over thirty years ago I took up my first teaching post in post-compulsory education, at an inner-city further education college, I had no real notion of what 'mentoring' involved. I certainly had no formally designated mentor. I did, however, find that it was possible to identify a number of more experienced colleagues who were inclined to be supportive, and with whom I felt comfortable sharing some of the professional uncertainties and anxieties I was troubled by. Looking back, I can view this situation as one in which I was actually the beneficiary of what we might call *distributed mentoring* – a small group of individuals were, wholly informally, playing an important part in my professional support and socialisation. Other relevant theoretical perspectives that I would now invoke are ones pointing to the utility of 'relationship constellations' and 'developmental networks' (Higgins and Kram, 2001), the latter being 'the set of people a protégé[1] names as taking an active interest in and action to advance the protégé's career by providing developmental assistance' (Higgins and Kram, 2001: 268). Of course in reality teachers will probably always seek informal – sometimes more formal – support from a variety of individuals, be they departmental colleagues, teachers in other institutions, former teachers or whatever. However, what is now virtually the norm across the post-compulsory sector, as it is in schools, is the designation of a named member of staff as someone who will be matched to a less experienced colleague, very often someone who is still in training, and be given substantial, formalised, responsibilities for their support and guidance. Inspection bodies and training institutions in fact *require* that this process take place, as I have alluded to in my Introduction. Mentoring is viewed as a fundamental dimension of the induction of new entrants to teaching, and it would be viewed as very poor practice for any college or other PCET institution not to have in place systems for organising mentoring; as a professional activity it has simply become a part of an experienced teacher's many and diverse roles.

With many more such teachers becoming involved in mentoring it appears legitimate to make a case that they too – initially at least – can benefit from support and guidance. With this aim in mind, what I have, therefore, attempted in this guide is the distillation of my own experiences as a teacher, mentor and teacher trainer, and insights from a range of texts and documents which practising mentors may not have the time, or inclination, to read in full. The perspectives, and practical guidance, that are offered have also, crucially, been shaped by the actual experiences and views of the large number of mentors and trainees who have shared these with me over many years. If it is still at all appropriate to write in terms of a 'theory/practice divide' in education, it is strongly hoped that this present contribution to enhancing mentoring will be viewed as falling on the practical side of such a line. Where I draw on selected theoretical perspectives (most especially in Chapter 3) I do so for the important reason that they appear to offer credible, helpful, insights to complement a 'good sense' view of mentoring. It is hoped, on the one hand, that the avoidance of an *in-depth* examination of theories of professional learning and of mentoring will not be judged to have resulted in too superficial an approach, or to strike readers as being merely a 'dumbed down' version of them; the risks in this regard are probably symptomatic of those run by 'academics' when addressing practitioners working in very demanding educational settings.

I fully acknowledge that mentoring is a professional transaction that can assume an almost infinite variety of forms. The 'contours' of the transaction, and of the relationship as a whole, will be moulded by the experience, educational philosophy, attitudes and personal style of both of the principal actors – mentor and trainee. Eliot Freidson (2001) argues convincingly that in fact professional activity cannot be standardised – that one of its defining characteristics is the way in which specialist knowledge is applied *with discretion*. If we accept this position, then logically we must appreciate that no two mentors will, or should, operate in precisely the same way. To add to this observation, I would need to observe that I cannot have first-hand experience of every single PCET institution in which mentors are working – although in almost two decades' worth of visiting colleges, adult education institutes, prisons, and very many 'off-site' and outreach centres I do have a reasonable degree of awareness of the sheer range of the possible settings referred to.

By offering certain important perspectives on mentoring it is hoped that a fuller range of potentially useful strategies can be drawn on than might be possible purely on the basis of intuition. Two of my principal aims have been to avoid dogmatism, and to examine the *why* (the 'point' of the activity as alluded to in my quotation from the novel *Now and Then* at the start of this chapter) as well as the *how* of mentoring, and in so doing to stimulate in readers a deeply reflective process focusing on the scope, purposes and limitations of the activity.

Mentoring does not take place in a vacuum, and for this reason I will attempt to contextualise the activity by introducing certain broader organisational and socio-cultural developments. There is much that is taking place outside of post-compulsory education that can usefully inform our efforts to further consolidate mentoring as a core activity in colleges and other PCET institutions; we need to engage with the professional challenge of doing so for very good reasons, one of which is simply that:

> Subject-specific skills must be acquired in the teachers' workplace and from vocational or academic experience. Mentoring, either by line managers, subject experts or experienced teachers in related curriculum areas, *is essential*.
>
> (DfES, 2004: 8; emphasis added)

This was at the time it was written a radical statement of intent, but is now, I would argue, embedded in our collective professional consciousness as a highly persuasive endorsement of the fact that mentoring cannot be construed as in any sense an 'optional extra' in the training of new teachers. The complexities and demands of PCET teaching have never been greater, and mentors have a key role to play in developing

> teachers who will be responsive to the diverse needs of post-14 learners and who are innovative, flexible and challenging in their practice [and who] are critical and reflective towards their own teaching and continuing professional development, committed to professional values and practice and to ensuring equal opportunities for their learners.
>
> (University of East London, 2010: 7)

Mentoring, like teaching itself, has at its core a 'trainable' set of skills, rather than being based purely on an innate disposition to help and nurture – such human qualities are highly desirable ones in a mentor, but in isolation from professional and practical knowledge and experience, and concrete ways to give trainees the benefit of these, their value is greatly lessened. What I am therefore attempting (in Chapter 2, for example) is to *link* mentors' professionalism and positive personal attributes with the many ways in which these can be actively deployed in the support of their trainees, so that the aspirations conveyed by the above statement from a major training institution can be realised.

Mentors will almost certainly be predominantly working with teachers enrolled on training programmes, on either a pre- or in-service basis. There are of course some major differences between these two types of courses (of which in purely numerical terms the latter is of greater significance in the context of PCET) but there are also many similarities. For example, a trainee on a part-time, in-service, CertEd or PGCE course who has been newly appointed to a college's staff may well experience as many uncertainties, and may well be as disoriented by the newness of life as a college teacher, as a recent graduate moving straight from university to a full-time one-year programme and only attending a 'placement' college for their teaching practice.

A new appointee will sometimes find they have almost as lowly a status as a 'student' teacher, in terms of such considerations as being able to influence departmental policies and practices. Longer serving – but previously untrained – college teachers may, on the other hand, experience special difficulties attached to finding themselves 'on the other side of the desk' for those parts of the week when they are attending their training programme. While many feel positive – excited even – about having been given the chance to formally qualify as teachers, others may perhaps feel a sense of grievance that their existing craft or academic knowledge is no longer seen as a solid enough basis on which to teach their specialisms. The latter group may in fact present particular challenges as far as mentoring is concerned.

Post-compulsory institutions[2]

As far as the institutional settings for the activity of mentoring is concerned, I have tried to take into consideration the needs of mentors who are working with trainees in settings as diverse as:

- General further education (GFE) colleges
- Sixth form colleges (SFCs)
- 'Land-based' colleges (LBCs), specialising in agriculture and/or horticulture
- Adult colleges and adult education institutes
- Community and outreach settings, e.g. hostels for the homeless
- Prison education
- Private training institutions, especially those delivering contracted or franchised courses.

I would contend that there exists a 'package' of trainable, generic, mentoring skills that it is possible to deploy in any of the post-compulsory environments listed above. A mentor gaining experience, and refining their skills, in a general FE college would be unlikely in my view to be overly daunted by the prospect of working in any of the other types of institutions in the list. Being most familiar with the first two types of institutions I have listed – especially the first, the GFEs – I have tended to draw my illustrations of mentoring and (teaching) situations from these; when I have used the expression 'the colleges' I have primarily had in mind both the GFEs and the SFCs.

Teaching in such settings has probably never before presented the range of challenges as it does at the present time. Even when writing in 1998, Jocelyn Robson observed that:

> The nature of teaching in FE has always varied enormously and continues to vary within the different curriculum areas. As the sector has expanded its provision, so its character has become more complex and the demands upon teachers have increased.

> (Robson, 1998: 591)

Today the situation is almost certainly significantly more professionally challenging, for the kinds of reasons discussed in the Introduction to this book. Three short extracts from the programme objectives[3] of just one training provider allow us some insight into what has become a fairly general consensus around the nature of certain of these challenges:

> On completion of the programme trainees will be able to:
>
> ... 6. Identify areas which may act as *barriers to learning* and devise strategies to address these in order to promote equal opportunities and an inclusive learning environment.
>
> ... 7. Differentiate teaching to meet the needs of all learners, including high achievers, those with a *history of educational failure*, those with learning difficulties and disabilities and those for whom English is an additional language.
>
> ... 11. Organise and manage the learning environment safely and effectively, including responding to *challenging behaviour.*
>
> (University of East London, 2010: 8; emphasis added)

From the above it is immediately evident ('history of educational failure', 'challenging behaviour') that college teachers are having to play a pivotal role in one of the segments of the UK education system that will call for a high degree of resourcefulness and resilience. The extracts add weight to the contents of such influential key documents as *Colleges for Excellence and Innovation* (DfEE, 2000), which some time ago now forcefully stated why it was that far greater attention should be paid to

> the development of the teaching staff, and senior management, in further education. It is they who are the essential resource who make the difference between learning which fails in achieving its objectives and that which is effective ... we [cannot] continue in a situation where too many further education teachers have no formal qualifications or where, in too many cases, professional development is still insufficiently embedded in a culture of continuous improvement.
>
> (DfES, 2000: 24–5)

The major survey report compiled in 2003 by OfSTED is essential reading for anyone wishing to identify a key point in the transition from the 'before' of (limited) teacher training for PCET and its present state. The report set out to review the quality of FE teacher training, and made a number of really quite critical observations: the summary of the report's findings actually begins by stating that

> the current system of FE teacher training does not provide a satisfactory foundation of professional development for FE teachers at the start of their careers. While the tuition that trainees receive on the taught elements of their courses is generally

good, few opportunities are provided for trainees to learn how to teach their specialist subjects, and there is *a lack of systematic mentoring* and support in the workplace.

(OfSTED, 2003: 5; emphasis added)

The importance attached to enhancing subject-specific mentoring in the sector was evident, and the recommendations made in this regard were unequivocally endorsed by the Standards Unit of the DfES in the following year (DfES, 2004). As can easily be imagined, the reverberations of the OfSTED survey have continued to be of very great significance in teacher training circles, but so too will they be for PCET institutions hosting or employing trainees, of course. Effective mentoring simply has to occupy a central position in the sector; we would be leaving far too much to chance, and making far too many assumptions about the natural talents and skills of new entrants to teaching within it, by adopting such a stance as one based on the premise 'well, s/he's doing a training course, isn't s/he?'.

Issues of quality and of student entitlement

Issues of quality in teacher training, of mentoring, and of teacher quality itself, are intrinsically related to broader concerns within the sector – especially 'the quality of the learner experience' it provides. Colleges, ever since becoming independent corporations almost twenty years ago, in 1993 (following the Further and Higher Education Act of 1992), have devoted a considerable proportion of their energies to raising quality and achievement levels, with virtually all conceding that doing so hinges, first and foremost, on their human resources, teachers in particular – the workers 'at the chalkface', 'on the front line' or those (especially since 1997) 'involved in delivering' to learners.

Richard Gorringe, in a much quoted phrase, once referred to post- incorporation colleges being in the business of 'attracting, retaining and delighting paying customers' (in Cunningham, 1997: 6), the customers of course being students. In the highly competitive, target-driven, environment in which colleges have had to operate ever since 1993, the aim of providing such services, which if not actually 'delighting' the student body at least meet their *entitlements,* has been absolutely crucial in understanding the ethos of post-compulsory education.

Such now 'vintage', but still important innovations as, first, a Charter for Further Education (DfE, 1993) and then the adoption by each individual college of its own Student Charter, laid out for prospective and current students what they could expect from their studies, and from the staff who would support them in these. Such documents provide, in effect, 'checklists' against which the actual experience of college life can be measured. Where there is a misalignment, i.e. where what is being delivered fails to match what has been promised, students are usually now actively encouraged to draw this to the attention of relevant staff and/or bodies. Mentors can, incidentally, very usefully provide trainees with a copy of their own college's charter (alongside the other kinds of materials detailed in Chapter 2); it can, fairly obviously, give a trainee insights into how their learners might be viewing, and evaluating, their performance.

There has been, as with most 'quality-related' initiatives which have impacted on PCET, some debate about whether the dawning of the Charter era has actually effected any really improvements in the student experience, or has merely signalled the arrival of another set of high-minded (if not always that elegantly expressed) 'ought to have' statements. Yet in a number of quite specific ways it is hard to argue with what most charters tend to say about, for instance, such matters as the nature of the grading and comments students can expect to receive following the submission of assignments. Who would quibble with an undertaking to learners that 'work is assessed regularly and promptly. You will be kept informed of your progress' (Coleg Glan Hafren, n.d.). The high degree of importance attached to speedy formative feedback on written work – say within a three-week period – is absolutely in line with sound educational thinking on such issues. Similarly, an emphasis on supporting students' *individual* learning needs is very strongly aligned with what research tells us enhances the quality of learning.

Most college prospectuses include explicit statements regarding what level of support tutors will provide for their students. We may perhaps feel that these sorts of documents may breed a 'culture of complaint', but viewed more positively they not only empower students but also serve to underscore what in the wider educational community is only seen as good practice. The strong relevance of all this to mentors is that their trainees may well need, and will probably benefit from, an element of their induction being focused on student entitlement as one highly important aspect of modern PCET.

With the advent of a much larger presence within colleges of the 14–16 age group, as new opportunities open up for school pupils in this age band to access the PCET curriculum (and as schools possibly become yet more assertive about excluding individuals whose behaviour is deemed to be disruptive to the learning of others) there will be many more issues arising, it seems likely, from college teachers being 'in loco parentis'. In such a context mentors will be yet further challenged to adequately support new entrants who may find that colleges are in fact very much more diverse environments than they might have presupposed.

Trends within professions, and society, generally

Mentoring in the school sector

The fairly obvious first place to start when reviewing developments in other professional areas is to look at the school sector, and make some comparisons with our own. Doing so has, arguably, a special value in the current climate of curricular change and the emergence of '14–19' as a key component of what comprises the UK education system. If there are approaches to mentoring being adopted in the school sector – which has a far, far better established tradition in this area – then we may well stand to profit from the sector's experience.

One very real difference between the school and college sectors is that very few teachers indeed in the former will be undergoing their initial training in-service, whereas this is the training mode that accounts for by far the greatest proportion of our own trainees. A second area of difference lies in the existence of formal 'probationary year' arrangements for new schoolteachers.

Such differences lead, for example, to a situation in which school-based mentors are often far more actively involved in the assessment of trainees' written and other tasks that they must complete before qualifying. The differences also mean that, at least for their first year of teaching (the 'NQT year', i.e. the newly qualified teacher year) new entrants have an actual entitlement to support and mentoring. These kinds of things mean that the 'jurisdiction' of mentors, as well as their status, is enhanced. In addition, it seems in general true that school-based mentoring is more likely to be incentivised both financially and in terms of career advancement. This last point has long been contentious among many mentors in PCET, who often perceive that their own willing involvement in mentoring is somewhat taken for granted.

Mentoring in other professional settings

Alongside what we can witness in the schools sector, however, it is worth mentioning, at least in passing, the kinds of trends evident in other spheres of professional life. In business and commerce, for example in an organisation such as the Royal Aeronautical Society (RAeS), mentoring principles and practices appear to be very fully embedded. The RAeS has adopted guidelines produced by the Engineering Council to produce its own guidance notes, to which it is clear that adherence by members is expected. These guidelines stress such facets of mentoring practice as 'developing a close relationship with [trainees] ... assessing them regularly, and ... providing tuition and guidance as necessary' (RAeS, 2001).

Mentors working to RAeS guidelines will work with three or four trainees at any one time, and are very strongly encouraged to 'remember there are other mentors' from whom learning can be derived, and to 'use the relationship for [their] own development too' (ibid.). So positive is this particular organisation's conception of the benefits of mentoring that the guidelines end with the note that:

> We encourage mentoring for at least two years of the trainee's career, but there is no reason why it should stop, and indeed it is preferable that *it should continue beyond that time*. If you both find the relationship worthwhile and rewarding then we would encourage you to continue to meet.
>
> (ibid.; emphasis added)

There seems to be much food for thought for the PCET sector in such a strong endorsement of mentoring, especially over a longer time period than is common in education. And it is not only in the organisation named here that mentoring has been given a high profile; the same situation is discernible in a growing range of other non-educational settings, and a book of this length cannot attempt to adequately describe this trend.

Mentoring in the community

We should also at least acknowledge the ways in which mentoring has been adopted by certain segments of the wider community to assist in the raising of standards and aspirations. The initiatives within black and minority ethnic (BME) communities are perhaps especially interesting ones. A number of these fall within the broad ideal of 'mentoring for social inclusion', or what has been described as 'engagement mentoring' (Colley, 2003: 2). This type of activity has focused on – as the term implies – preventing young people's *dis*engagement with school and/or society, or *re*-engaging those who have already, in one way or another, 'dropped out' as a result of their disaffection or inability to progress. As a variant of mentoring it has relied heavily on volunteers, and has been strongly associated with the kinds of outreach in the 'non-participant' community promoted by governments since at least 1997.

It is such a 'community' that was depicted in a poster campaign mounted by a north London local authority endeavouring to reduce the incidence of car crime: 'male mentors' were sought to work with young men at risk of beginning the anti-social – and highly dangerous – activity of 'joy riding'.

Each of this small number of illustrations simply serves to show how the diversity of contexts in which mentoring is now being encountered is large, and is growing. Even within colleges themselves, alongside the type of mentoring on which this guide necessarily concentrates, we may find in existence such variants on mentoring as:

- student 'buddy' systems (i.e. peer mentoring);
- the mentoring of current students by previous, successful, ones;
- mentoring by representatives of academic institutions (usually universities) aimed at promoting applications from underrepresented groups;
- employers assisting potential new recruits' readiness to successfully confront their selection procedures.

Mentors to teacher trainees are not therefore alone in devoting a portion of their skills and energies to supporting the learning and development of others. Mentoring is an area of rapidly growing importance and interest and in certain respects appears, certainly in the context of teacher training and development, to be an excellent case of 'an idea whose time has come'. 'Mentoring is far more than a fad' according to one source (Johnson and Ridley, 2004: p. xv) and another has quite famously gone even further in contending that 'everyone needs a Mentor' (Clutterbuck, 2001).

An 'architecture' for mentoring

To return to our own specific context, I would want at this point to introduce some propositions that I believe are of major importance in exploring the kinds of factors that can impact within PCET on whether mentoring can fulfil its true potential as a supportive, and ultimately professionalising, strategy. I have, since the first edition of this book appeared, elaborated elsewhere (Cunningham, 2007) on what I describe as the kind of 'architecture' needed for mentoring to thrive. Here I will try to summarise some important elements of the notion of architecture, in the hope that doing so will illuminate for practising mentors why they may feel in varying degrees either supported or constrained in those aspects of their professional work calling for them to support teachers in training. Being somewhat provocative, it may be that in some small way I will prompt among mentors the motivation to adopt elements of an *activist* (Sachs, 2003) teaching professional, and to endeavour to campaign for improvements in their own institutions' architecture.

Whether or not we would accept the validity of the observations with which the foregoing section is concluded, in particular that *everyone* needs a mentor, I would argue very strongly that *effective mentoring needs solid institutional backing*. Many analogies or metaphors would be possible here – from the 'fertile seedbeds' out of which mentoring might 'grow and develop', through the right 'climate' in which mentoring will 'thrive', to 'powerful motors' which will 'propel mentoring forward'. Having encountered and considered a number of such notions, I feel that none offers quite as much scope for describing and addressing mentors' needs within the organisations in which they practise as that of an 'institutional architecture'; this can encompass issues ranging from quotidian practicalities to far-reaching strategic matters, I would claim.

As well as attempting to point to some useful definitional components of mentoring, and alluding to its potential for endowing professional benefits on both parties involved, we should, therefore, consider the institutional conditions – or *architecture* – likely to be conducive to the activity. This is a worthwhile exercise, for a number of reasons, but one in particular: as well as planning to identify and enhance individual capacities for mentoring it is essential to consider how institutional capacity will be supportive of the activity. Furthermore it also seems fairly self-evident that if mentors are thinking about the 'ought' of mentoring (as in *what ought to be in place to support them*) they will be better equipped to lobby, as I have hinted, over any marked institutional *deficiencies*.

For mentoring to be most effective within an organisation, the individuals involved need to be adequately supported by what we might then conceive of as the *architecture* surrounding the activity. Put simply, the term as I use it here describes those 'design features' that support rather than constrain the work of mentors. In the same way that so-called 'sick' (i.e. badly designed) buildings are sometimes held to be responsible for lack of productivity, poor staff morale, high levels of absenteeism, etc. so too might an organisation lacking the appropriate architecture be prone to ineffective, under-resourced and under-valued mentoring.

A number of key factors can be considered to be involved in ensuring that mentoring takes place within a well-designed environment – an organisation where 'the architecture is right'. Although the post-compulsory sector is an extremely variegated one, containing a great diversity of places of learning and training, it nevertheless appears possible to identify certain factors of generic, overarching significance and some of these are summarised below.

An institutional commitment to mentoring

Mentors must believe that their efforts are recognised and rewarded. This, at a very basic level, would probably entail their being given a small amount of release from their own weekly classroom (or management) commitments. More positively, an involvement in mentoring might be a criterion for consideration in connection with promotions, or the award of 'advanced skills practitioner' status or similar organisation-specific designations. PCET institutions might additionally very strongly promote the potential of involvement in mentoring activities to form an element of practitioners being able to supply evidence appropriate within the context of the Institute for Learning's (IfL) '30-hour rule' regarding their continuing professional development (CPD); mentoring is actually a particularly valid form of CPD, for a number of reasons, not least of which is that the professional development of at least one other person besides the IfL member themselves stands to gain. And fairly clearly the gains are even more extensive, in that the institution is facilitating the dissemination of good practice, and thereby – without, I hope, overstating a case – enhancing the quality of learners' experiences.

An appropriate institutional ethos

The term 'collegiality' has probably become somewhat overworked but the promotion of a collegial climate is certainly relevant to our notion of an appropriate architecture for mentoring. As a notion, collegiality has the real merit of encompassing the potential *reciprocity* of mentoring relationships. Mentors make their knowledge and skills available to less experienced colleagues but in turn learn from them, too. Mentors' professional learning can be enhanced by the kinds of questions posed by trainees ('Yes, but why do you think that would be a useful strategy to use with this group?') and by the kinds of scenarios they are likely to present for discussion ('So what would you have done in that kind of a situation?'). Mentors' understanding of their own professional practices and the legitimacy of these can only be deepened by the kinds of interaction alluded to here. Institutions would do well to take opportunities – e.g. in recruitment literature and staff handbooks – to make explicit the ways in which they are seeking to foster collegiality through mentoring.

A second valuable construct that can be drawn on with reference to the value being attached to mentoring is that of 'communities of practice' (Lave and Wenger, 1991). In the classic formulation of what is involved in such an entity, and using the perhaps rather daunting terminology 'legitimate peripheral participation', Lave and Wenger describe how:

> learners inevitably participate in communities of practitioners and … the mastery of knowledge and skill requires newcomers to move toward full participation in the sociocultural practices of a community. 'Legitimate peripheral participation' provides a way to speak about the relations between newcomers and old-timers … It concerns the process by which newcomers become part of a community of practice.
>
> (Lave and Wenger, 1991: 29)

For 'learners', in our present context we can conceive of these as being the trainees, without in any way, it seems to me, distorting the authors' original perspective. An institution actively promoting the development of a community of practice, and focused interaction between 'newcomers' and 'old-timers', is one highly likely to achieve 'full participation' by the former group, I would contend. One of the ways in which Lave and Wenger add to our understanding of how learning takes place – for our purposes *professional* learning – is that they give special emphasis to the social, and in doing so open up a broad range of opportunities for institutions to develop communities of practice, rather than limit their strategies exclusively to those bounded by classroom walls.

Using somewhat similar terminology to 'communities of practice', the Department for Education and Skills described the advantages of 'creating "professional learning communities"[4] in colleges and providers' (DfES, 2004). Here, too, we have an endorsement of the importance of its *ethos* in the *effectiveness* of a college or other PCET institution.

Some PCET institutions have so strongly taken on board the importance of mentoring within their overall human resources policies and procedures that they have even produced a *mentoring policy*, with such documents frequently making plain how this articulates with certain other important guidance statements such as their:

- quality assurance policy;
- induction procedure;
- recruitment policy;
- staff development policy and procedures;
- staff review policy and procedures; and
- equal opportunities policy.

The advantages of thereby integrating mentoring within a wider set of 'architectural features' of the organisation are potentially very great; certainly there is minimal risk, it would seem, of mentoring being perceived by staff as in any way peripheral to the college's mission.

The physical resources for mentoring

Basic minimum requirements here would include the availability of a – preferably dedicated – meeting room in which such confidential activities as post-observation debriefings can take place. Mentors might also use this room as a venue for periodic discussions or occasional 'case conferences'. It might also be the most appropriate location for the kind of action learning sets whose functions I describe elsewhere in this book.

In some institutional settings, electronic networking by mentors might be more realistic than face-to-face meetings, so facilitating this (e.g. by recommending use of college intranets) should be prioritised. Similarly, institutions' financial resources might allow for the purchase of a small collection of relevant texts that mentors could borrow, and/or subscriptions to worthwhile professional journals; where they do not, then dissemination of information regarding subscription-free access to relevant electronic journals and newsletters is of course appropriate.

Induction, training and support for mentors

The skills set needed by effective mentors should not be considered to be exactly the same as that displayed by *all* good teachers; there are certainly important overlaps, but no institution should take for granted the readiness to begin mentoring of even highly successful classroom practitioners. Induction of new mentors is essential (and of course is one further way in which institutional commitment to the endeavour can be communicated to staff).

The first dimension of induction should ideally comprise a clear articulation of the *rationale* for mentoring – how it accords with an institution's mission, its strategic plan and how it should be viewed as fundamentally connected to 'the learner experience'. The centrality of the learner within the current inspection framework makes it essential that the role of mentoring in, ultimately, enhancing achievement is highlighted in the induction of mentors.

Also deserving of a prominent place within the rationale being presented for mentoring is an indication of how the activity will possibly be viewed by other actual or potential 'stakeholders'. Here we are considering the value of having a sound mentoring scheme in place should there be external scrutiny in connection with such awards as Investors in People, or the various quality 'kitemarks' which are seen, rightly or wrongly, in the PCET sector (and elsewhere) as being worthwhile indicators of a healthy, successful organisation.

The kind of training provided at the induction stage should be underpinned by sound theoretical perspectives relevant to the activity of mentoring, but should also benefit from the inclusion of case studies, where these can be derived from teachers' professional biographies, and clearly indicate the credit which mentoring can be given for any improvements in professional practice.

It would be possible to write in great detail on the structure and content of mentor induction/training, but here I would only wish to highlight one additional highly desirable feature of such events. This is the prominence that would need to be given to classroom observation, given the undoubtedly increasing significance of this aspect of their roles which mentors will discern. (I devote Chapter 4 to the question of approaches to classroom observation).

Induction should only, however, be seen as the first stage in the support of mentors and it will need to be supplemented by ongoing support. Such support can take the form of providing opportunities to share not only issues and concerns, but also successes and best practice.

In the contexts of both induction/training and ongoing support, there may well be an argument in favour of engaging external trainers/facilitators, rather than having senior staff take responsibility for organising and delivering events. It is possibly less likely that negative sentiments might be generated when outside contributors are used ('management sermonising, then trying to use mentors in a surveillance operation to weed out weak teachers …'). But this is a highly debatable supposition, it has to be acknowledged.

The selection and accreditation of mentors

But who are the staff to be inducted and trained as mentors? A useful perspective from the context of the school sector is that 'mentoring only flourishes when it's perceived by senior managers as an important aspect of staff development rather than a tiresome burden to be landed on unwilling and unprepared shoulders' (Stephens, 1996: 4). We can, I hope, see the equal validity of this proposition when translated to colleges. First, therefore, mentors should ideally be selected, rather than 'landed with' the role, and here we arrive at one of the greatest challenges to institutions seeking to have their 'architecture' properly thought out. The post-compulsory sector appears recently (in particular since 1993) to have suffered disproportionately from poor morale, a perception by long-serving staff that the pressures of teaching have been greatly added to by the growth of an intrusive 'audit culture', by the advent of student entitlements and by the ever-increasing diversity of the cohort. Furthermore, we are aware of a degree of 'innovation fatigue' being experienced by staff as one proposal for curriculum or accreditation reform seems to follow another.

In this difficult climate, the heart of the challenge is in portraying mentoring as a desirable, worthwhile activity with both personal and professional rewards attached to it. A starting point for constructing such a positive, attractive, profile for the role ought really to start with the drawing up of appropriate selection criteria, making it plain that status and kudos will accrue to individuals able to meet these. Institutions also need to actively seek arrangements with training providers and/or awarding bodies that would allow for the accreditation of mentoring as a high-level work-based professional activity. Already HEIs with important interests in the post-compulsory sector allow for the accreditation (most typically at master's level) of such professional learning as derives from mentoring, with registration fees sometimes being paid by employing organisations in the sector.

By signalling such possibilities as these, the professional benefits of mentoring for mentors themselves, as well as trainees, are heavily underlined. As with certain other aspects of institutions demonstrating their commitment to mentoring, as outlined above, these kinds of initiatives seem to depend as much on will, and priorities, as on financial resources.

Issues of clarity and consistency

These two considerations are most sensibly reviewed together, as they are strongly interconnected. First, it seems self-evident that in the same way as selection criteria for intending mentors are necessary, so too is a clear specification of what exactly the role entails; mentoring needs a job description, in other words. What are the principal functions mentors are expected to fulfil, with what kind of frequency, and what kinds of documentation (if any) will they have to deal with? Similarly, if mentors' obligations – and their entitlements – are being spelled out, so too should be those of trainees.

The nature of mentors and trainees' responsibilities, and the divisions between these, can even be embodied in a mentoring *contract* – which in its most formal guise would actually be signed by both parties, perhaps. This kind of device allows for easy reference to the key dimensions of the mentoring relationship as being proposed within an organisation, and it can fulfil the very important function of elucidating the boundaries within which both parties are agreeing to act.

Whatever format is adopted for outlining 'who does what' (or ought to), it should ideally embody a set of ideas based on a *shared ownership* of these. A sometimes lengthy but ultimately worthwhile process is to establish a small working group of individuals from various levels of an institution to draft guidelines on which mentoring relationships should be founded – for evaluation after a specified period in use. This to a reasonable degree can militate against criticism of what is being proposed, and in particular will pre-empt the claim that any new procedures have merely been 'imposed by the management'.

While we must acknowledge that an overly rigid approach to the structure of mentoring could in itself be a factor promoting antagonism to any scheme, clearly a high priority aim must be to ensure a good measure of consistency across departmental/ curricular areas. A model of an overarching framework – or contract – setting out responsibilities and entitlements for both mentor and trainee would be one in which there was some scope for 'good sense' flexibility and adjustments. But it would also have in-built guarantees of *minimum* levels of contact, support, observation and so on, no matter what the trainee's specialism. This can help ensure that any sense of grievance which emerges, where say a trainee feels they have not been provided with the same level of 'face to face' time as a colleague has had with another mentor, can be discussed with reference to, and framed by, what has been approved as institutional policy by a number of stakeholders. Guidelines for good mentoring practice, to be readily discerned by their readers as promoting consistency across subject areas, must of course be written in an accessible way, must avoid ambiguity (whilst retaining the flexibility I am advocating) and should be regularly updated in the light of experience and evaluation.

In principle, the aspiration of trainees to be mentored by someone whose area of expertise closely matches their own is not hard to accept. There seems little doubt that not only do statutory bodies wish to see subject-specific mentoring arrangements in place, so do trainees themselves. Wherever feasible, therefore, mentoring by a co-specialist (or at least by someone from a disciplinary background cognate with that of the trainee) should be engineered. However, it is probably unrealistic to establish absolutely hard and fast rules on the matter in a number of institutions. Some may have tiny specialist departments, where the 'newcomer' (see above) is perhaps the only full-time member of staff. Elsewhere, literally no appropriately experienced staff within a department or section may be available.

In these kinds of problematic situations there appears little to recommend beyond attempting to negotiate mentoring by someone from another discipline, to be supplemented where possible by arranging access to subject-specific support outside of the institution – e.g. in one of the subject groups/centres publicising their activities in special interest journals.

However, it is also well worth reminding ourselves at this point of two things. First, that of course all trainees will benefit from 'being introduced to wider professional issues' (Lucas, 2004) and secondly of the risks attached to professional learning 'being ghettoised into narrow, subject-based notions of teaching' (ibid.). In the very restricted domains of some vocational areas it is quite possible that 'narrow ways of teaching have become entrenched' (ibid.): for this reason if for no other we would probably be mistaken, therefore, to seek a panacea for all the present perceived deficiencies in institutions' mentoring arrangements in the shape of subject-specificity.

Measuring the impact of mentoring

For any claims to be made at all about the effectiveness of a mentoring framework which has been put in place there needs to be some mechanism for researching this – for gathering data and making sense of it. This, then, is the last but by no means least important dimension of an 'architecture' for mentoring to which some thought needs to be given.

If post-compulsory institutions are to become 'learning organisations' (which some, without a doubt, already are), then they need to investigate every aspect of their practices. The current emphasis on self-evaluation, as required by the inspection framework for the sector, is of course of strong relevance here. Within the specific context of mentoring, however, the demands for data and analysis appear to be minimal. Therefore a fuller picture should probably be sought, perhaps by such key personnel as those with major staff development responsibilities. Pursuing such a course can only lead to a better understanding of the components of effective mentoring practice. Logically, it will be most productive as a course of action if data are gathered from mentors, trainees and their supervisors/managers. Further, it has special potential to inform the kind of mentoring to be conducted in cases of teacher underperformance (such as surface because of student complaints, typically) where the price to be paid for ineffective, poorly targeted, mentoring can be a high one. Evaluation and monitoring of mentoring should actually produce the kind of concrete 'continuous quality improvement' now long promoted across the sector, but especially in cases where teaching standards and learner achievement are causing concern (Kingston, 2004).

References

Clutterbuck, D. (2001) *Everyone Needs a Mentor: Fostering Talent at Work* (3rd edn), London: Chartered Institute of Personnel and Development.

Coleg Glan Hafren (n.d.) *Student Charter* (3rd edn), Cardiff: Coleg Glan Hafren.

Colley, H. (2003) *Mentoring for Social Inclusion: A Critical Approach to Nurturing Mentoring Relationships*, London: RoutledgeFalmer.

Corlett, W. (1995) *Now and Then*, London: Abacus.

Cunningham, B. (1997) The failing teacher in further education, *Journal of Further and Higher Education*, 21/3: 365–71.

Cunningham, B. (2007) All the right features: towards an 'architecture' for mentoring trainee teachers in UK further education colleges, *Journal of Education for Teaching*, 33/1: 83–97.

Cunningham, B. (2008) 'Learning Community', in G. McCulloch and D. Crook (eds), *Routledge International Encyclopedia of Education,* London: Routledge.

DfE (1993) *The Charter for Further Education*, Nottingham: Department for Education.

DfEE (2000) *Colleges for Excellence and Innovation*, Nottingham: Department for Education and Employment.

DfES (2004) *Equipping our Teachers for the Future: Reforming Initial Teacher Training for the Lifelong Learning and Skills Sector*, Nottingham: Department for Education and Skills.

Freidson, E. (2001) *Professionalism: The Third Logic*, Cambridge: Polity Press.

Higgins, M. C., and Kram, K. E. (2001) Reconceptualising mentoring at work: a developmental network perspective, *Academy of Management Review*, 18: 56–87.

Johnson, W. B., and Ridley, C. R. (2004) *The Elements of Mentoring*, New York: Palgrave Macmillan.

Kennedy, Dame Helena (1997) *Learning Works: Widening Participation in Further Education* (The Kennedy Report), Coventry: Further Education Funding Council.

Kingston, P. (2004) More colleges fail in south, *Education Guardian*, 30 November.

Lave, J., and Wenger, E. (1991) *Situated Learning: Legitimate Peripheral Participation*, Cambridge: Cambridge University Press.

Lucas, N. (2004) When there are too few mentors in the pot, *Times Educational Supplement*, FE focus, 21 May.

OfSTED (2003) *The Initial Training of Further Education Teachers: A Survey* [HMI 1762], London: Office for Standards in Education.

RAeS (2001) *Guidance for Mentors*, London: Royal Aeronautical Society.

Robson, J. (1998) A profession in crisis: status, culture and identity in the further education college, *Journal of Vocational Education and Training*, 50/4: 585–607.

Sachs, J. (2003) *The Activist Teaching Profession*, Buckingham: Open University Press.

Stephens, S. (1996) *Essential Mentoring Skills*, Cheltenham: Stanley Thornes.

University of East London (2010) *Cass School of Education PGCE (PCET) Programme Handbook, 2010–2011*, London: University of East London.

Mentors' skills, attributes and functions

Chapter objectives

- to specify the core activities of mentoring, and the most appropriate attributes and skills for undertaking these.

Teachers change in countless ways during the process of their careers ... They become more experienced, at least in the sense of having taught for a longer time. They often learn new skills. They do things better. They become more knowledgeable ... They sometimes become more patient, wise and witty. Some of them, however, become discouraged, fatigued, 'burnt out', cynical, lazy. A few of them go dotty.

(Philip W. Jackson)

Yes, but what exactly is my mentor supposed to be doing?

(Anonymous trainee teacher)

The first of the above quotations (from 'Helping Teachers Develop', in Hargreaves and Fullan's excellent *Understanding Teacher Development*, 1992 – still a source of real value to all observers of teaching) nicely draws attention to the wisdom and patience that fortunate experienced teachers acquire over the years. These two attributes are as valuable as any mentors are likely to possess. On the other hand, one would hope that most practising or intending mentors are not afflicted by any of the negatives which are mentioned – although who has not experienced a natural fatigue after a full day's teaching into which a great deal of energy has been put? Possessing positive *attributes*, or 'dispositions' is an enormously important foundation for the development of mentoring *skills*. What I shall focus on in this chapter, however, is not only these skills and attributes but also how they come into play in the actual job of mentoring – performing the wide range of functions attached to the role.

The second opening quotation (one of very many similar that I might have used) draws our attention rather abruptly to the fact that, at least for trainees themselves, what precisely such functions might include is not always entirely understood.

Mentoring: definition and specifications

Most mentors would probably quite readily be able to note down a few points they would work into an explanation of what exactly it is they feel they have taken on. However, it would probably be surprising if at this early stage some kind of working definition of the activity were not provided, and I would therefore propose the following:

> Mentors in PCET are skilled, experienced teachers who are involved in guiding, counselling and supporting trainees in practical ways. They are able to offer both a role model and essential information on a college's learners, its curriculum, its organisational structure and its policies, at least those relating to learning and teaching.

Clearly this is at one and the same time a definition more tightly focused than one to be found in a dictionary (e.g. usually something along the lines of 'wise teacher') and significantly different from one relating to the specifics of a different occupational area – many of which tend to stress 'coaching' as being at the heart of mentoring. It is, incidentally, important to observe that in a number of regards trying to draw meaningful boundaries between the activities of mentoring and coaching is arguably not all that productive: they overlap greatly, and for two authors at least the term *mentor-coach* is what seems most appropriate (Pask and Joy, 2007).

Many training institutions adopt more succinct versions of what is involved in mentoring trainees, the University of Cardiff, for example, simply stating that 'a mentor will be an experienced subject specialist and a classroom teacher' (Cardiff University, 2003). The Further Education Training Organisation emphasised in its materials, during the lifetime of this body, that a mentor should be 'an excellent teacher … [who] can encourage others towards excellence' (FENTO, 2001: 1), seeming to indicate ways in which mentors ought to actually *stand out from* other practitioners. A best-selling text on teaching in the PCET sector opts for the equally to the point: 'an experienced member of staff who provides ongoing support, advice and guidance' (Huddleston and Unwin, 2007: 185). A number of colleges are themselves of course also involved in the delivery of initial teacher education and they have attempted to define what mentoring entails (as have some colleges not so involved, but which are nevertheless putting staff mentoring schemes in place).

So, there is a range of possible ways of encapsulating what mentoring comprises, and it would probably be fruitless to try to identify any one perspective on the activity as being superior to others. Largely as a result of the very large number of professional spheres in which mentoring has been initiated (and subsequently researched by academics) it is exceptionally difficult, in fact, to claim that any one definition has an all-encompassing, comprehensive, validity. Some years ago, Healy and Welchert (1990) described a 'definitional conundrum' arising from a tension between classical notions of long-term (often spontaneous and based on goodwill) mentoring relationships, and those which are 'on the other hand … assigned, short-term, cost effective arrangements of limited significance' (Healy and Welchert, 1990: 18). While it is clear that virtually all the 'arrangements' which readers of this guide will be concerned with will generally fall into this latter category, they can certainly possess, however, *very real significance – for both parties.*

Given the prominence which is given in initial teacher education to *reflective practice* (see Chapter 3) it seems only logical to highlight early on the strong desirability of mentors themselves being in sympathy with the notion. Reflective practitioners are very probably also those endowed with the wisdom and patience Jackson refers to. They are the experienced teachers who still, after however many years, mentally review classes they have taught, are sensitive to things which did not go as well as they wanted them to, and are constructively thinking ahead to implementing refinements. The mentor who is a reflective practitioner will be most able to empathise with trainees' anxieties, I would contend, because they remain far from complacent or blasé about their own performance in the classroom; in short, they have *not* stopped reflecting on, and learning about, teaching. They manifest some of the important attributes of *learning professionals* (Guile and Lucas, 1999).

At the risk of standing accused of veering too far into the realm of popular psychology, it may also be the case that effective mentors are individuals whose 'emotional intelligence' (as a great number of writers are now referring to a particular set of perspectives; see e.g. Goleman, 1999) is well developed. They are not only self-aware regarding their own feelings – what antagonises, or what hurts, for instance – but are adept at gauging how their words and actions will be reacted to by others, that is, in the present context, by trainees they are mentoring. They are, to put it simply, sensitive and considerate; they also find it possible, emotionally, to accommodate without distress a view of the world which may be at odds with their own. Alongside seeking to effect change and improvement in their trainees they are themselves open to change in their own attitudes and behaviours, accepting that the professional learning arising from a mentoring relationship may not be an exclusively unidirectional process.

Effective mentors are also very probably the kinds of individuals who would fall within Hoyle's highly influential conception of *extended professionals* (Hoyle, 1974), teachers who embrace involvements with professional activities beyond those of teaching in their own classrooms (in contrast to the group Hoyle defined as *restricted* professionals). They may, too, be inclined to assume *activist* (Sachs, 2003) roles – for example, rigorously advocating for their trainees in various quarters, or campaigning for the creation – where it does not already exist – of the kind of 'architecture' described in Chapter 1.

All of the above notions may, perhaps, point to the existence of a 'mentoring mindset', but in certain respects some of them are simply what we can recognise as the defining characteristics of any person-centred professional activity. Mentors, most especially new mentors, will probably though – and entirely understandably – focus more on the practicalities of what will be required of them than on contemplating these ideas, and useful sources of guidance here are first the materials provided by teacher training institutions, principally universities (and increasingly by colleges themselves), and secondly the expectations of new trainees as they emerge as a result of academic research. There is little to be gained here by attempting to summarise in any useful way what trainers are currently stipulating: each mentor will need to adhere closely to the specific requirements of a particular training scheme. However, some recently expressed views of trainees themselves may provide a helpful depiction of the kinds of expectations with which mentors can be faced.

'What trainees say they need'

Certain themes may be seen to emerge from a collation of anonymous responses gathered by me over a four-year period (to 2004) to questions posed to trainees regarding what they hope a mentor will provide for them, and what facets of mentoring they view as essential. The kinds of perceptions held are shown below; to avoid a large amount of repetition many responses from the trainee cohorts concerned are left uncited, but, as indicated, the most important themes can be illustrated on the basis of those statements which are used. There is no particular priority implied by the order in which the list has been compiled.

- 'genuine concern for my development';
- 'support and encouragement';
- 'I hope my mentor is, most importantly, a good teacher whom the students respect and who I can be inspired by and learn from';
- 'will give me continuous feedback whether good or bad';
- 'somebody who will keep me involved from the outset, and make clear what is expected of me';
- 'someone who takes a genuine interest in me as an individual, as well as a trainee;'
- 'approachable, and willing to give constructive criticism';
- 'consistent support, structure and guidance';
- 'will set me realistic and achievable aims';
- 'someone who will be friendly, and put me at my ease in a new environment';
- 'an understanding of my abilities, strengths and weaknesses';
- 'comfortable about expressing opinions about what I can do to improve';
- 'subject-specific help about how to present particular topics'.

One thing which may well strike readers is the degree of openness conveyed by a number of these verbatim statements; there is plentiful evidence of willingness to learn, and a real acceptance of the fact that criticisms from mentors will form part of the transaction. Trainees are, I would contend, overwhelmingly receptive to being mentored. High value is being attached to the services of a mentor, a starting point that would be hard to improve on – but one that may occasionally be experienced by mentors as somewhat daunting.

Trainees' anxieties

To complement these kinds of statements regarding trainees' *needs*, it might be useful at this point to attempt to raise mentors' awareness of the kinds of *anxieties* they frequently bring with them. Again, I present here only a relatively small selection of the kinds of issues raised anonymously in similar exercises, and over a similar period, as those which produced the statements in the list above. Nevertheless, they are highly representative of the recurrent themes we encounter when researching how trainees experience their situation as beginning teachers.

- 'Being assessed, e.g. teaching the class and being observed on my performance then graded';
- '[Teaching] groups of mixed ability and motivation';
- 'I hope I will be sufficiently knowledgeable in my subject area to be able to teach it to the required standard';
- 'I hope I can stand up and teach in front of a room full of people';
- 'I am concerned about how much time we will have to prepare our first lessons once we know what subject matter it is we will have to teach';
- 'A little frightened about my own knowledge [and] questions that students might have – not being able to answer immediately';
- '… concerned about maintaining a high level of self-confidence';
- 'I think I'm going to look younger than most of my students';
- '[Getting] a good job at the end';
- 'Standing up and presenting material. Does it get easier?';
- 'Generating interest and a stimulating, animated, classroom environment from dry, theoretical, subject matter'.

These, then, are the sorts of things – the needs and the anxieties – around which mentors will want to devise appropriate supportive strategies. In doing so, their own skills and attributes may sometimes allow them to take this in their stride; at other times (and in particular in the context of the problem-focused mentoring dealt with later in this guide) they may feel really quite stretched. Possessing the kinds of 'CV items' described below will undoubtedly be a solid foundation, one that can be built on over many years of mentoring practice.

A 'CV' for mentoring

Mentors working in the specific context of supporting trainee teachers will ideally be endowed with a range of skills such as those described below. As will become evident, the list strongly corresponds to one that could be collated on the basis of the kinds of sentiments and perceptions of trainees that have been summarised above.

Proven effectiveness in the classroom

Skills in this area may not exclusively have been judged on the basis of exam results (although these may well be taken into account by managers seeking to identify prospective mentors). Other highly relevant measures of effectiveness can be said to include student satisfaction as indicated by evaluations and surveys, retention rates and – more subjectively – simply the kind of credit and esteem colleagues tend to confer when someone becomes known as an engaging and popular teacher. It might be that the classroom skill and expertise of a mentor has already been acknowledged formally within an institution, and they may for example hold 'beacon', 'champion' or 'advanced practitioner' status (all designations currently being encountered, among others).

Management skills

The term here is being used in a very broad sense, to encompass such areas of professional life as course design and management (often taken to include seeking accreditation for or verification of a programme, oversight of exam entry procedures, organising the purchase of relevant course materials, etc).

Mentors who are adept at file management, coping with the demands of a 'data-hungry' environment, and who have an ability to remain unperturbed by deadlines – and to meet them – may also be advantaged, because undoubtedly the mentoring function carries an increment of paperwork attached to it, in the forms of reports to be submitted by advised dates and so on. All phases of education are now in their own slightly different ways *audit cultures*, and being able to peacefully coexist with this fact, if we cannot embrace it, is important.

The ability to form and maintain effective professional relationships

This dimension of mentoring lies at its very heart. To support and enhance the professional development of a trainee entails, at its most basic level, being able to get on with them and encouraging them to feel positive about working with a mentor.

> As with many of the roles that support experiential learning, it succeeds or fails on the basis of the relationship that is established between the mentor and mentee.
>
> (Fry *et al.*, 1999: 145)

There is, of course, a risk attached to stressing, in a guide such as this, 'relationships'; the term can connote an emotional intensity, loyalty and commitment which are very rarely, if ever, going to be as appropriate in mentoring as they would be in certain other contexts. Nevertheless, the justification for referring to the notion is easily located in the frequency with which *unsuccessful* mentor–trainee 'pairings' are described by trainees in the language of 'failed', 'bad', 'negative or 'unhealthy' relationships.

Some, at least, of the positive characteristics of good personal relationships probably do have a transferability to mentor–trainee ones – mutual respect, reliability, honesty, tolerance of failings and a measure of flexibility all come to mind.

High-level communication skills

'He knows his subject, but really gets in a mess trying to say what he wants to say.' In certain essentials, mentoring draws on key *teaching* skills: the mentor is coaching, advising and guiding 'their' trainee. These activities, to have successful outcomes, all call for such staples of the teacher's repertoire as being able to pitch information at an appropriate level, avoiding pretentious or jargon-ridden expositions, and actively inviting requests for restatement or clarification where necessary. All good teachers also place emphasis on what is most significant, are self-aware of any potentially offensive phrasing (whether culturally, socially or sexually, for instance) and are alert to the risks posed by ambiguity.

As the educationist Lewis Elton often expresses it when identifying what is at the heart of effective teaching, it is the ability of the expert to *translate* their knowledge in such a way as to make it accessible to the uninitiated. This simple concept not only ought to inform our teaching in the most fundamental of ways but seems to offer a great deal to an understanding of the nature of effective, positive, mentoring.

An ability to counsel

In another educational context, that of personal tutoring, Waterhouse (1991) presents a strong case for this activity depending on a mix (shown in his original text as a somewhat 'tennis court'-like diagram) of skills borrowed from both teaching and counselling. I would argue quite strongly that a similar proposition has validity when applied to mentoring. From the traditional set of *teaching* skills mentors draw on their ability to describe and explain, to set out alternatives, to underline the significance of certain facts and principles, and so on. From *counselling*, they find themselves, for instance, using their listening skills, empathising with difficulties being experienced, and supportively drawing out what trainees might actually be feeling (perhaps sometimes in contrast to what they *say* they are feeling?).

It is not in any sense being implied here that mentors need to have pursued a course of psychotherapeutic counselling training before they can be considered qualified to assume their responsibilities. (And of course it needs to be noted that there are actual dangers in attempting to be 'real' counsellors to our trainees without having had the benefit of such training. The issue of *professional boundaries* very strongly comes into play in this regard.)

I am simply indicating that certain basic, strongly humanistic, elements of counselling practice can be of value to mentors in their work. As teachers, very probably many in fact already do possess well-honed listening skills and are ever-receptive and attuned to their learners' anxieties. It is highly likely that the majority of practising mentors have previously held responsibilities as personal tutors to learner groups, and many will continue to work in this setting while also mentoring. It is, therefore, simply the probability that mentors will connect with a 'tutoring-derived' model that leads to its inclusion here.

Strong subject knowledge

The present overwhelmingly *generic* nature of much training for the post-compulsory sector is clear. Against this backdrop, the very special and highly valued contributions of the subject specialist cannot be overrated. The designation 'curriculum mentor' adopted on some training schemes in itself signals the distinctiveness of the role

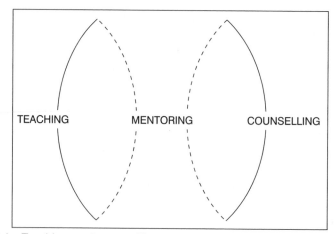

FIGURE 2.1 Teaching and counselling: overlapping skills for mentoring. Adapting Waterhouse's representation of tutoring skills (1991: 8) to a mentoring context

and its responsibilities. The terminology 'subject co-tutor' is one that would give even greater prominence to the desired subject-specificity of mentoring; although previously this has primarily been favoured within the context of training for the school sector, the post-compulsory sector has had to devote far more attention to the matter in recent years.

Being an expert in one's subject allows for much more than, say, simply being able to tell a trainee that there has been an inaccuracy in some factual material they have been teaching – which is not to dismiss the importance of doing so where necessary. Subject expertise, combined with length of teaching the subject, means that mentors can provide inputs which it is highly unlikely trainees will get access to in other quarters. In particular, mentors ought in principle to be able to do the following.

- Recommend the most up-to-date and valuable sources of subject knowledge which trainees can draw on. Such sources can encompass texts, professional journals, electronic sources, and courses/conferences.
- Offer advice, on the basis of experience, concerning which elements of topics/texts/assignments have tended to cause learners most difficulty. This will enhance the ability of trainees to target their efforts, both in the classroom and when designing and producing learning materials, so that special emphasis is given to supporting learners in areas which have apparently often presented barriers to learning.
- Provide insights into such practical considerations as how much time it has been demonstrated learners ought to spend on the various parts of a syllabus to ensure success.
- Induct trainees into the specifics of relevant accreditation in their subject, so that trainees can confidently approach the business of preparing their learners for major assessment hurdles. For mature entrants to teaching in particular,

the differences between the organisation and 'badging' of examinations now and, say, in the 1980s are often perplexing and they will tend to need a lot of support in understanding the present landscape of credentials and assessment strategies.

■ Allow access to their own classes, so that the observation of teaching becomes a two-way process. Trainees can learn a vast amount from the observation of a skilled, experienced teacher of their own specialism – seeing the pacing, pitch and style of a professional teacher at work is a priceless opportunity, and one in fact which will probably come about only extremely rarely in the first years of a new entrant's career in PCET.

■ Simply sharing their enthusiasm for their subject, and demonstrating that it isn't inevitable that after a given period staleness and cynicism set in!

It is, finally, worth reiterating that an even greater emphasis is being placed on subject-specificity in mentoring as the reforms comprising the government's Success for All agenda are highly consequential for mentors. Now being sought are: 'in particular approaches to mentoring to help teachers develop teaching skills *in their own specialist or subject area*' (DfES, 2004: 4; emphasis added). While the contributions that can be made by generic mentoring (e.g. as offered by trainees' personal tutors) are acknowledged both by teacher trainers and in recent policy documents, it is undoubtedly the role of subject-specific mentoring that is now in the ascendant. There has been in evidence a far more formalised set of responsibilities for colleges to organise the recruitment, training and support of mentors from across the post-compulsory disciplines if they wish to be part of partnership arrangements with training providers.

Core responsibilities of the mentor role

As I have already indicated, each training institution will almost certainly set out in its own course-related documents the range of responsibilities (and sometimes entitlements) which mentors will have. Some of the possible specifications for mentors' activities – the requirements and boundaries of the role – are illustrated by the brief extracts from just one training scheme which are included below; clearly it is compliance with these which ought ultimately to inform how to approach working with a trainee. As would be evident from perusal of a larger sample, there are not huge variations in the ways in which mentoring is conceived by individual institutions; it would probably be somewhat puzzling if this were not found to be the case. Certain consistencies emerge, most of which are wholly concordant with those principles and practices advocated in the literature of mentoring. It is not therefore all that worthwhile to examine at any length what the numerous training institutions have specified, and the following 'snapshot' should suffice to give a flavour of current conceptions of the remit of mentors.

Cardiff University when describing, for example, the purposes of regular mentor–trainee meetings holds that these should be structured around opportunities to:

- discuss classroom experiences with a view to making teaching and learning more effective;
- focus on strategies to promote effective teaching and learning as appropriate to the subject;
- promote critical reflection on practice (Cardiff University, 2003).

Mentors working in partnership with this particular scheme are advised to organise their meetings with trainees on a fortnightly basis. They are also advised that to complement their own observations of a trainee's developing practice they should liaise with those subject teachers being released from their normal class contact by virtue of groups being temporarily taught by trainees. (Thus, incidentally, the recent requirements for additional observations can be complied with, as well as allowing a mentor to more effectively monitor classroom performance.)

Besides regular meetings and conducting observations, mentors attached to this scheme are typically also involved in

- monitoring the lesson plans trainees produce;
- writing reports and references;
- giving attention to the 'constraints and requirements' of such aspects of college life as external examinations;
- advising on the design and production of learning resources; and
- overseeing how trainees are planning to embed and develop Key Skills within their teaching (ibid.).

The mentoring 'mix'

Both from the above sample guidelines, and from various guidance provided later in this chapter, what may well become evident is the fact that mentoring new college teachers encompasses not only providing certain wholly practical forms of assistance but some far less tangible, 'psychosocial', contributions to trainees' well-being and development. The mix might be said to be linked to the 'hard' and 'soft' skills, respectively, which are sometimes held to be involved in all professional life. Writing an observation report draws on the 'hard' skills of accurately reporting what went on in a class, and doing so within an acceptable time frame and sensible word length. But it also requires the 'softer' skill of being able to imagine, and empathise with, the reader's response to the report – especially, of course, if it is one containing essential criticisms. Some mentoring activity will be most strongly dependent on mentors' 'hard' skills (including their subject-specific expertise), while at times their softer skills – their very nature, or dispositions – will come to the fore.

The mix of what is entailed in mentoring is apparent from the very earliest stage of a mentoring relationship with a new trainee. The new entrant to college teaching has a range of immediate practical needs, and will seek a mentor's help in meeting these – finding out what departmental resources are available is an obvious such *practical* issue. Other concerns of the new entrant may in fact be far more *emotional* in origin and nature. Under this heading, there may well be quite pronounced, basic, anxieties about survival:

> The survival theme has to do with reality shock, especially for teachers with no prior teaching experience, in confronting the complexity and simultaneity of instructional management: preoccupation with self ('Am I up to this challenge?'), the gulf between professional ideals and the daily grind of classroom life, the fragmentation of tasks … The list goes on.
>
> (Huberman, 1992: 123)

In other accounts of trainees' early preoccupations (e.g. Cunningham, 2000) the fact that starting teaching is indeed a daunting transitional state is fairly clearly evident, and interestingly it seems almost uncorrelated with the maturity of the trainee. A newly recruited trainee on a pre-service course once wrote (anonymously): 'I'm very aware of how relatively young I am, and how much I still have to learn, and have trouble seeing myself as someone who has the authority/experience to teach.' Yet trainees with twenty or thirty years' industrial or commercial experience, and numerous accomplishments in their field (individuals who are, of course, often especially valued as new entrants to teaching), are not immune from their own distinctive concerns (including, notably those concerning ageism) as witnessed by, for example, 'Can an old dog be taught new tricks [while] adapting it all to family life?'; an anxiety anonymously aired, on paper, at the same time as the preceding one.

Mentors will, therefore be concerned with operating in various ways, practical and otherwise, to ease the passage of trainees into a sector of education which has never previously presented quite such a range of professional opportunities and challenges as it currently does. In such a context, it would perhaps be unsurprising if at times the litany of mentoring functions takes on a resemblance to the *'lipsmackinthirstquenchin…'* Pepsi Cola advertisement:

> teaching, coaching, advising, guiding, directing, protecting, supporting, sponsoring, challenging, encouraging, motivating, befriending, inspiring, *esteembuildinrolemodellinformationgivinskillssharincareerdevelopinnovicenurt urinrisktakingradeimprovinaspirationraisinhorizonbroadenintargetsettinkingmak ingmakinselfregeneratincriticallyreflectinperformanceassessinfeedbackgivin* …
>
> (Colley, 2003: 31)

To avoid this blurring effect, however, what I would argue we must do is focus primarily on the specific actions – and their desired effects – which can feasibly be incorporated into the very restricted amount of regular contact between mentor and trainee which most real-world college 'architectures' will allow for.

From their major survey of the mentoring literature, Johnson and Ridley 'distilled' what they found into

> 57 key elements for effective mentoring … clustered around six primary themes – what excellent mentors do (matters of skill); the traits of excellent mentors

(matters of style and personality); arranging the mentor–protégé relationship (matters of beginning); knowing thyself as mentor (matters of integrity); when things go wrong (matters of restoration); and welcoming change and saying goodbye (matters of closure)

(Johnson and Ridley, 2004: pp. xiv–xv)

This 'further distillation' as we might term it, seems to be a useful one, succinctly encompassing *activity* and *chronology* as well as the *personal* and *interpersonal*.

Another attempt (and there have been very many) to locate what exactly lies at the heart of effective mentoring was that of Anderson and Lucasse Shannon (1995). They describe as the 'essential attributes' of such mentoring

(a) the process of nurturing, (b) the act of serving as a role model, (c) the five mentoring functions (teaching, sponsoring, encouraging, counselling and befriending), (d) the focus on professional and personal development and (e) the ongoing caring relationship.

(Anderson and Lucasse Shannon, 1995: 29)

Particularly helpful, I feel, are two *dispositions* which they also draw attention to, namely 'opening ourselves' and 'leading incrementally' (ibid., p. 32). The latter notion encapsulates very well the idea that mentors cannot expect their work to be immediately transformative but must, most often, aim to be the overseers of a *gradual* process of a trainee's skills development and gaining professional confidence. It appears wholly unrealistic to expect that trainees will become fully integrated, expert, members of a community of practice within just a few weeks.

However, closer, more-specific *links* with our trainees and their professional sphere will still need to be made, which is the purpose of what follows. As noted earlier on, much of the body of literature from which the foregoing samples have been extracted is not remotely concerned with PCET, deriving as it does from studies based in a wide range of occupational areas. We must, though, aim to find ways in which mentoring will be most effective within the college setting – drawing where appropriate on perspectives from other areas of professional activity when these do seem to have a real transferability.

Narrowing the focus

There is a set of core functions and responsibilities which can be specified for college-based mentors and which is, in some respects, timeless. By this I mean that no matter what the prevailing educational policies are, the nature of student cohorts or the stage we have reached in the development of available educational technologies, there will exist an underlying set of trainee needs. Mentors will be involved in trying to meet these whatever the externalities presented by an ever-changing educational environment. By being attuned to the nature of the changes taking place, however, they will be able to deliver mentoring with modernity. The first specific function outlined below offers a good example of how, in a sense, the timelessness of certain needs can coexist with some of the wholly ephemeral, transitory, aspects of present educational structures and systems, and in particular the discourse being generated by these.

'Jargon busting'

For new and 'newish' entrants to college teaching one of the most daunting initial hurdles to overcome is becoming familiar with the enormous number of terms and abbreviations which post-compulsory education has spawned, especially since the early 1990s. It can be a dispiriting, excluding, situation to be in where staffroom and social exchanges among experienced staff are dominated by language unlikely to be immediately accessible. College teaching, like all professional occupations, has what linguists would call its own 'sociolect'. This derives from such sources as:

- the range of descriptions applied to learner groups;
- curriculum policies and changes;
- other relevant legislation;
- college policies, procedures and documents;
- subject-specific language, etc.

I have attempted to show in the simple diagram (Figure 2.2) how we can sensibly view all this as essentially being related to certain 'scales', from the micro (i.e. individual student in their classroom) to macro (major social changes driving government policy). Each box of *discourse*, to borrow another term from sociolinguistics, nests inside a larger one, as in a Russian doll. Illustrations of what may be found within each 'box' are then given below. These, however, will almost certainly be supplemented during the life of this guide; some may become obsolete, and the current meanings

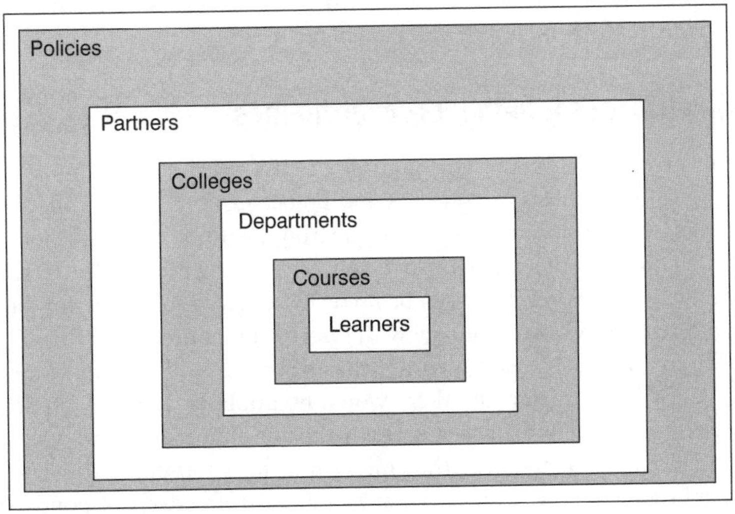

FIGURE 2.2 The sources of jargon in colleges

attached to a further group will perhaps have changed. It seems, therefore, wisest to be thinking in terms of a changing inventory of terms, acronyms and abbreviations which in mentors' own judgement could usefully be explained as opportunities arise.

In this collation of sources of jargon, some illustrations of specific terms arising within each nesting box might include:

- *Learners:* statemented; link student; ALS [additional learning support], etc.
- *Courses:* abbreviations relating to examination boards/awarding bodies; portfolios; criteria; specs. [specifications], etc.
- *Departments:* abbreviations relating to titles of these and key personnel within them such as HoD [head of school]; 'Grade 2' (or other number) as a shorthand for departmental quality as judged by OfSTED. etc.
- *Colleges:* abbreviations relating to key personnel such as VP [vice principal]; site names where a college is 'split site'; terms used to designate special functions of parts of the premises – 'helpdesk'; SAR [self-assessment report]; etc.
- *Partners:* governors; names/abbreviations for institutions with which franchising arrangements exist.
- *Policies:* Leitch, etc. [referring to the various key Reports]; Kennedy [referring to the widening participation initiatives arising from this specific Report]; MAs [modern apprenticeships]; etc.

What is clearly essential, just as it would be in mentors' own classrooms, is to promote an ethos in which 'it's OK not to know', and saying 'just ask if there's anything which doesn't make sense' is an integral part of the mentoring repertoire. Mentors should be reassuring that being bemused by the jargon of college life, the evolving qualifications structure, etc., is not an inadequacy, and is something which can quite speedily – almost always well before the end of a PGCE/CertEd – be got over. It is, though, hard to overstate the importance of inducting trainees into this aspect of the professional world which is the college sector today, to enhance the confidence with which they will encounter it.

Inducting trainees into the 'broader themes'

Being provided with the right language ('PCET-speak'?) is of course only one side of the equation. The major concerns and preoccupations of the college sector have an actuality which impacts on new teachers from their first day on the job. Trainees are of course taught about a range of such concerns during the PGCE/CertEd programmes they attend. However, there can be no really adequate substitute for direct encounters with certain issues, and dialogue with informed mentors about these.

We could probably each identify what we conceive of as some of the present 'really big issues' in the sector, and there would no doubt be a fairly high degree of overlap between what one practitioner sees as of major importance, and what another would highlight. There could well (but might not) be a consensus that engaging with the issues in Table 2.1 is essential, so that we can most effectively respond to the challenges they present.

TABLE 2.1 The 'big issues' in the sector

• Reducing social exclusion, and widening participation in higher education
• The nature and requirements of external inspection
• A major shifts in interest away from 16+ and towards 14+ transitions
• Far greater attention given to the inclusion within mainstream education of those with additional learning needs
• Growth in student entitlements, and the concomitant onus on institutions to demonstrate their responsiveness to 'student voice'
• Focus on personalised learning and achievement rather than on attainment of groups as a whole
• 'Quality'–related initiatives and the growth of an audit culture
• The prime importance of student retention
• Increased competition between education providers in 'marketised' local environments
• The expanded professional roles and responsibilities of teachers
• Overriding management anxieties regarding funding allocations

The listing is, as I acknowledge, one which might not be exactly replicated by other observers of recent changes in the post-compulsory sector, but any variations might not be too startling. It is quite possible that some would add to the list such other discrete items as the Every Child Matters agenda, gendered gaps in attainment, and elearning. On the other hand, if we really do start to see more of the promised local collaborative, e.g. consortium-type, arrangements among providers than exist at present then an item in Table 2.1 such as 'Competition' could be deleted ...

It would be hard (and probably unnecessary) in a guide of this length to detail the implications of every issue proposed here as being of significance, and to describe for each one a set of strategies which mentors might adopt to allow trainees to more easily make connections between the issues or developments and their own experiences. But it is the business of *making links* between the items in the list and the placement or employing college which is important, not making an attempt to 'begin at square one' and, in didactic fashion, lecture trainees (which will be happening elsewhere, almost certainly). For the present, illustrations of how mentors may guide and support their trainees in one or two areas might, however, be of value.

Student entitlements

Developments here do, of course, *visibly* connect with what has been witnessed in at least two other areas, namely, increased competition for students since the early 1990s, and the recent importance attached to debates over colleges' ability to retain students once they are recruited. There are no doubt strongly altruistic elements involved in a drive to ensure that students are getting a fair deal from a college, and from their teachers in particular: it would be deeply cynical to fail to recognise this.

Yet it is only balanced to suggest that colleges need to ensure that entitlements are met so that the potential for student withdrawal, complaint or actual litigation is greatly minimised. No college could afford the damaging effects on its local reputation which would result from a publicised complaint about a failure on its part to meet a student's entitlement, or to provide a 'quality learning experience'.

At a basic level mentors can simply provide trainees with whatever documents or statements are supplied to students in which their entitlements are set out. They can provide additional guidance on the nature of the 'constructive formative feedback' that such documents usually promise students. They can, similarly, exemplify what precisely was meant within the institution when a statement relating to 'regular individual tutorials' was framed. They can very strongly promote in trainees the merits of encouraging their learners always to raise any concerns with them before reporting them in other quarters. And, in worst-case scenarios, mentors may offer to intervene/act as mediator should an 'entitlement' issue between a trainee/learner (or learner group) not appear to be susceptible to a straightforward resolution. (Sometimes, if this stage is reached, it may emerge that a particular learner has been falling down with regard to *their own* responsibilities, while claiming their entitlements have been unmet.) Overarching all of these possible actions, though, there is, yet again, the need to ensure clarity regarding the rationale for student entitlements, and to display a positive attitude towards this aspect of the current educational scene.

Quality and audit

It would quite easily be possible to write a book-length review of issues under this heading, indeed someone is probably doing so at this very moment ... Stephen Ball has written particularly persuasively on the ways in which audits and *performativity* have fundamentally affected the preoccupations of teachers (Ball, 2008). There is often a marked degree of negativity flavouring discussions of quality assurance procedures ('Kwality' as one columnist in the educational press would often derisively refer to it) such as 'internal review/audit', and the very much greater emphasis being placed by managers on teachers' compliance with requests for various forms of student- and course-related data. The terms 'paperchase' and 'paper trail' have become fairly commonplace, and the proposition that teachers sometimes seem to spend as much time documenting their teaching as actually teaching is encountered in not a few staffrooms. In my own experience, both trainees and recently qualified new teachers perceive the whole area as being, in general, daunting and demotivating. 'I don't think anyone ever reads any of the stuff anyway' is the kind of sentiment quite routinely expressed concerning much of the documentation that must be supplied in the name of quality assurance. Or, as Ball expresses it rather more elegantly: 'We make ourselves calculable rather than memorable' (Ball, 2008: 56).

So, how much of value can mentors hope to bring to such a situation? There appear to be both 'philosophical' and practical inputs which might be supportive ones for trainees. In terms of the former, it may for example be very worthwhile to point to the available evidence relating to retention and achievement: although there are pockets of poor performance in the sector, some colleges are performing very well indeed, and *overall* (in terms of numbers of students achieving their target qualifications) results have been steadily improving (Kingston, 2004). While we could not legitimately attribute all of this improvement to closer scrutiny of teachers' work, and more rigorous, in-depth, quality assurance procedures, some elements of it have very probably derived from the more prominent position 'quality' now occupies on most colleges' agendas. Close monitoring of results across curriculum areas has sometimes allowed for additional resourcing, and targeted support for the professional development of staff. The use of value-added analysis, and benchmarking (just two of the tools now available to us when researching quality issues) has indicated areas where achievement levels are not concomitant with what might be expected of a cohort. To veer into a discussion of retention, the much greater efforts put into finding out why students are expressing dissatisfaction or withdrawing have similarly allowed us to put together a picture of where exactly we need to be enhancing levels of learner support, or better supporting teachers in continuing to develop their skills yet further.

These kinds of things can be presented as positives, as can – at a more practical level – the merits of maintaining up-to-date schemes of work, full records for individual students and so on – the sorts of data virtually all colleges' management information systems will require. Compiling a bank of lesson plans seems especially easy to justify to trainees as being worth the effort expended: such a resource ultimately becomes an investment, and an eminently transferable one at that – with the necessary updating it might well serve a teacher usefully in a subsequent post. The sheer professionality of having taken the time to properly design learning sessions should be promoted – as well as the sense of security which can come from teaching a, perhaps challenging, group on the basis of a sound set of learning objectives/timings/activities – rather than relying on the 'note on the back of an envelope' approach. Mentors perform an especially valuable service for trainees when they take an interest in their developing planning skills, and praise any strong efforts in this area that they witness.

What mentors are actually doing when engaging in dialogue on these issues (and providing assistance in practical ways) is *accelerating* the professional learning of their trainees. Training programmes are relatively brief, and can offer but a 'précis' of some of the key features of the PCET environment; to more speedily and confidently be able to appreciate these fully, trainees will almost invariably benefit from a mentor's targeted inputs.

'Day-to-day realities'

In some ways, it is possible to conceive of a 'mentoring *syllabus*' comprising both coverage of the kinds of issues outlined above (focusing in particular on how they are impacting locally) and many other far less weighty but nevertheless important matters (see below). The notion of a syllabus might seem to contradict what was put forward in the Introduction – that mentoring as a professional activity is far from mechanical, and should be informed by discretion. But it would only be mechanistic if an absolutely rigid, inflexible, chronology and sequencing of 'topics' were to be proposed. Quite obviously some items will need to be dealt with at a much earlier stage than others. But beyond making this point it is probably true that each individual trainee's support needs will be different, dependent on their prior experiences – which may, for instance, include having worked as a teacher on a voluntary basis – their confidence and resourcefulness and their other personal characteristics.

It is probably going to be useful, in the above context, to systematically record what has been discussed at each of the regular meetings (probably weekly, perhaps fortnightly) which mentors will hold with their trainees – what ground has been covered, and how it is proposed to follow up things. Here, incidentally, is one of the numerous ways in which mentoring or supervision meetings might be likened to the individual tutorials we offer to learners (where these are based on their individual learning plans, rather than being events triggered by personal crises of one form or another, or, say, infringements of disciplinary codes).

Other key dimensions of the mentoring role that are worth underlining include addressing certain practical considerations which may seem entirely mundane – banal even – but do have a very strong impact on the ease with which trainees can acclimatise to college life. It is probably artificial to attempt to intellectualise about the kinds of practicalities dealt with in this section, beyond saying that we will be promoting the development of the kind of confident 'artisanry' that flourishes 'when things go well, when the routines work smoothly [leading to] a rush of craft pride that translates into what has come to be called "self-efficacy"' (Huberman, 1992: 136).

A mentoring 'toolkit'?

Although much of what follows will clearly relate mostly to trainees on pre-service courses, or to new appointees, we do all need to be confident that a range of essentials to do with 'housekeeping' and college procedures are dealt with. In certain respects, to borrow an idea from Napper and Batchelor (1989), dealing with these is most efficiently accomplished where mentors have organised for themselves a 'toolkit' of aids. The contents of this would differ from college to college, and between curriculum areas, but it might well include:

- a staff handbook;
- a student handbook;
- a package of exam board specifications relating to the courses offered within the relevant curriculum area;
- samples of past question papers and/or project briefs;
- summary notes relating to available departmental resources;
- any group or individual learner profiles which have been produced (although trainees usually have to produce these for themselves, to comply with one course assessment or another);
- guidance on the all-important photocopying (see below);
- keys or 'swipecards' where appropriate.

Mentors should themselves have been supplied with such items as a programme handbook for the specific training course a trainee is following, with key reporting documents – teaching observation proforma and the like – either contained within this or provided separately; this constitutes essential reference material for the mentor as opposed to those listed above, which clearly are for sharing with the trainee.

It is also important that mentors make explicit to trainees (that is, those not actually employed by a college itself) that *registers* and various other documents essential for college administration have to be dealt with alongside 'just teaching'. These are vital pieces of paperwork, not only for funding reasons of course but, e.g., in connection with monitoring student performance where individuals are 'on report' or whatever. It is wise to prepare trainees for the kinds of situations where students will approach them with attendance slips for signature by the teacher, for instance. The use of electronic registers has caused problems for not a few trainees, and it would be wrong to assume that everyone will find these completely straightforward.

Some other particularly frequently encountered issues, for which possession of a 'toolkit' may be a useful basis for action, are set out below.

Photocopying issues

Trainees may well not have a clear view of what it is, or is not, legitimate to request under the heading of *teaching resources*. The photocopied handout remains such a staple of our learning resources mix that photocopying always seems to throw up a number of problems. In an age where environmental awareness has become of such importance, the *sustainable* college can be conceived of not merely as one that lives within its financial means but its 'ecological' ones. (It is highly likely that young new entrants – those whose schooling has mostly been within the compass of 'greener' times – will be even more attuned to such important considerations than their usually more mature mentors.) Each college will have its own arrangements and stipulations for dispensing photocopying entitlements, and questions arising from this – absolutely crucial – issue might include:

- What is the maximum number of photocopies for my classes I can have per term?
- Do I need my own personal card/code to make use of the copier?
- Must I record anywhere the number of copies I am making?
- If I make too many copies does this reduce the total available for other members of the department?
- What are the arrangements regarding paper for the copier if the supply runs out while I am using it (and can I legitimately request help with loading this if I run into difficulties)?
- Am I allowed to use existing stocks of photocopied sheets in a departmental resources bank, and if so must I assume responsibility for replacing these?
- Should I simply be advising my classes to download and print materials for themselves?

As with many other such apparently trivial questions, even the half dozen or so above does not exhaust the range of possible queries. It has, in my experience been a major source of frustration for trainees who on occasion, beleaguered by learner groups about 'getting the handouts', have neither the confidence nor knowledge of a college's systems to know how to respond appropriately.

These kinds of matters are ones which, of course, will not in the slightest degree usually stretch mentors' knowledge and awareness of what is 'correct' in the context of a specific institution. While it may appear tedious to deal with them, this possibility is, however, offset by the smoothness with which various practicalities will become non-problematic for trainees.

Keys/swipecards to rooms, 'staff access only' corridors, etc.

I will argue below that in a fundamental sense, trainee teachers' identity as new members of a community is at least in part contingent on whether they have been given full access to the various items that 'proper' teachers usually take for granted. All educational institutions have necessarily become greatly more security conscious in recent years, with the use of student and staff identification and swipe cards becoming commonplace, for example, and much more emphasis on the need to 'please keep doors locked when rooms are unoccupied'. Most college staff, and legitimate visitors, have few if any criticisms of this trend – though they may of course lament the circumstances which have given rise to it. However, for a trainee, especially one on a pre-service course and therefore not having *employed* status, special problems may arise, in particular with regard to the matter of not being in possession of the necessary keys/cards. Some situations they find themselves in may lead to embarrassment, or loss of face in their eyes vis-à-vis how they are perceived by learners.

One example of what I am describing is as follows. We all promote the kind of professionalism signalled by arriving early at the room in which a class is to be taught, allowing for any sensible rearrangements of furniture, checking IT hardware, etc. before a lesson. If rooms are in continuous use – i.e. one group leaving as another enters – then the problem of having to locate keys doesn't arise. However, if trainees will with any regularity at all be teaching in rooms which will have been locked for security then they really do need to either be provided with keys or swipecards or know where exactly they can be accessed or borrowed. This is one of those apparently very minor issues which is in fact of real significance. Relations between trainees and their groups can be quite adversely affected by the kind of 'messy' start to a lesson which not being able to get into a classroom often results in. If, on eventually getting into a room, it is found to need substantial tidying up then this can lead to a situation, especially with more challenging young groups, where an unsettled, perhaps noisy, start can breed further disruption. (And a room simply *left* littered and/or with its furniture all over the place really isn't a conducive learning environment.) At the very least, given the reduced course hours syndrome which has been witnessed, the amount of time lost from teaching can be a cause for concern.

To make for a smoother experience for both trainee (and learners) the availability of keys/swipecards is then an important consideration. For the pre-service trainee it can add to their very sense of *belonging* to have their own; one element of being 'not just a student'. I have repeatedly witnessed the diligence with which trainee teachers wear or display their 'staff' ID cards, sometimes in contrast to what is observable amongst individuals one knows to actually be 'staff': there does seem to be a message here, one about responding positively to trainees' anxieties not to be viewed as outsiders – or 'just student teachers'.

ICT equipment, including audiovisual facilities

The hardware of most modern classrooms can cause a large amount of needless stress when it is either inaccessible (e.g. because log-in codes have not been provided to trainees), is broken or has gone missing. Well organised, generously resourced, college departments will usually employ the services of full-time, dedicated support staff monitoring the availability and serviceability of ICT/video etc. equipment, but this situation is possibly not universal, especially as far as supporting the teachers of evening or weekend classes is concerned. Mentors should prioritise performing such supportive tasks as demonstrating to trainees how a classroom's computer, data display board(s) etc. need to be used. They might mark, with 'Tippex' or whatever, the room number in which a video remote control should remain. They need to clearly communicate to trainees what has to be done if assistance with any of the technology is needed; is there an internal phone to contact relevant support staff, for example? Far more importantly, though, they should take as a guiding principle that trainees will generally be grateful for, rather than patronised by, the offer of pointers and assistance in connection with some of what is now the basic technology of classrooms.

Most trainers and observers of teaching will have witnessed the distraction and sometimes actual distress which trainees can experience when thwarted, in front of a group of learners, by 'simple' things. Anything we can do to militate against this is time well spent.

Flip chart holders/pages

While many teachers are far more reliant on Smart, or 'Promethean' boards than they are on more low-tech classroom aids, another very basic matter which has, however, the potential to cause a quite disproportionate degree of inconvenience if it is overlooked concerns the availability of A1-sized flipchart pads, which still remain in fairly frequent – if sometimes rather wasteful – use in classrooms. It can be a very rapid process indeed to use up a pad. With some classroom activities, e.g. small-group work, especially where it calls for the results of activities to be summarised by students on flipchart sheets, this tendency can be exacerbated.

Besides taking the obvious step of pointing out the need for a measure of economy – flipchart pads are surprisingly expensive – mentors can usefully ensure that the location of replacement pads is known, because almost certainly the question will arise. If a department allows or encourages the products of student work as written up on A1 sheets to be attached to classroom walls another common request from trainees that can be pre-empted is for 'BluTak' (or similar products), so that this can easily be done without causing permanent damage.

'The right kind of pen'

It is particularly easy to take for granted that trainees will know which pen/marker is correct for which medium/surface. We do, though, usually need to spend some time running through the importance to a trainee of checking the labels on pens, as well as letting them know where to find what they need.

Whiteboards – and far worse, Smartboards – can be quite seriously damaged by use of markers other than the 'dry-wipe' kind, and the ill-will this can generate amongst colleagues as well as the expense to an institution is worth pointing out. Trainees need some succinct advice on what to do if the whiteboard or Smartboard board in a classroom has – usually in spite of a large warning notice – been written on with a fluid proving hard if not impossible to remove. If no flipchart holder/paper (see above) is available as an alternative this kind of thing can cause much irritation and stress.

'Can I move the room around?'

In certain teaching contexts – the laboratory, say, or the computer suite – there are of course extremely limited opportunities for room rearrangements. (It may sometimes be possible and desirable to, say, ask learners to move their wheeled chairs away from computer workstations and towards the front of the room to listen to short 'whole-group' explanations). In most non-specialist classrooms, however, for sound pedagogic reasons we might want to encourage trainees to adapt room layouts for specific types of lessons. Discussion/seminar work is obviously best conducted with 'horseshoe' or semicircular seating arrangements, to facilitate eye contact, seeing which member of a group is making a particular point, etc. The 'committee' layout is said to work best for whole-group simulations, and 'café style' for small-group or pair work. And largely didactic sessions, or ones including a high proportion of individual work on tasks, can more often than not be run satisfactorily using the traditional 'rows' layout.

What is self-evident, based on the results of very many observations of practical teaching, is that a mismatch between room layout and the nature and purpose of teaching is a recipe for disaster. It is *nearly always* best if room rearrangements are allowed, *but* for the sake of goodwill we must stress the importance of returning classrooms to the layout in which they were found. Teachers with 'majority use' of a classroom can be especially affronted by temporary, unwanted, rearrangements and their position should be properly considered. Similarly, we should always encourage trainees to try to ensure that their learners don't leave too much debris in rooms for others to deal with, another potential source of discord which is fairly easily avoided. These kinds of areas may, I acknowledge, appear to be entirely trivial from certain perspectives – yet a reference request on my desk at the time of writing, from a high-profile sixth form college, asks for my comment on whether a candidate for a post 'keeps areas tidy and attractive' … The orderliness of learning environments is surely a motivating factor both for teachers *and* their learners.

Arrangements to do with accompanying or leading educational visits

It is of course a very valuable part of a trainee's experience to be involved with curriculum-related trips, and purely 'social' ones involving groups of students. Largely for reasons strongly associated with a number of tragic mishaps which have occurred on school or college trips (and the almost inevitable litigation which has ensued from these), all PCET institutions now need to be much more aware of their responsibilities with regard to such matters as:

- staff/student ratios when off the premises;
- appropriate certification as appropriate (first aid, approval for minibus use, etc.);
- parental permission in respect of 14–19 learners; and
- procedures in connection with necessary expenses incurred.

In general, agreeing to a trainee on a pre-service course assuming prime responsibility for planning and leading an educational visit is not to be recommended. Trainees who are actually employed by a college need to be especially fully cognisant of the contents of the institution's *risk assessment* procedures, given their contractual obligations to comply with such published guidelines.

Trainees and learning materials

All trainees will need to be guided and supported in matters to do with the core function of being able to select and develop resources to support learning. As one university expresses the point, trainees on completion of their programme must be able to:

> [8] Prepare and use high quality teaching and learning resources, using ICT as appropriate in the curriculum area.
>
> (University of East London, 2010: 8)

In the real world of most college settings, this activity will still generally include a very significant focus on text-based materials – handouts and worksheets in particular. However, designing materials for the specific purpose of making them available to learners via virtual learning environments (VLEs) is also now a key aspect of most teachers' roles. Mentors will be serving trainees' interests well if they, first, encourage experimentation with such materials; this is especially so as the great majority of training providers will be seeking evidence in their trainees of an independent and creative approach to designing materials. In environments where learners' attendance patterns are unavoidably erratic for one reason or another, having high-quality materials easily accessible on a college VLE becomes an especially important means of ensuring support for those whose studies are 'gapped'.

Clearly, however, it will not in general be advisable to promote the use of newly designed learning materials without these first having had the benefits of being commented on by mentors. As with many aspects of the mentoring relationship, what is not advocated is any kind of 'vetting' of trainees' performance in an area of teaching, rather the provision of *opportunities* for the discussion of, in this case, materials that are being proposed for use with a learner group. Perhaps most importantly, mentors can use their experience and insights in the following ways.

- Advise on whether the language level adopted on a sample of material is well aligned with the linguistic abilities of the group for whom it is intended. Might a glossary of topic-specific terms be a valuable addition to a handout, for instance? Are sentence constructions over-long? Is the phrasing of any of the questions/instructions ambiguous or too culture-specific (an extremely common fault seen in a high proportion of early attempts made by trainees)?
- Tactfully point out spelling and grammatical errors (which learners will more often than not tend to reproduce in their own work!) and reiterate what is sadly true, that computer 'spellchecks' cannot ever identify all of these. Current requirements in relation to a 'minimum core' level of proficiency (equivalent to Level 2) in literacy, numeracy and IT for all trainees adds some weight to the necessity for mentors, where appropriate, to devote effort to ensuring standards in these areas are acceptable: doing so will not be pedantic, simply professional.
- Make useful suggestions for promoting interactive use of the materials: what must learners actually *do* with what they will be provided with, beyond simply filing it? Have useful exercises been suggested, are there gaps in information which will require learners to usefully engage in research (or other activity) so that these can be filled in? Are there any pointers to further reading? Has the material been set in context, i.e. connected in some way to a specific part of a course?

Mentors will, of course, be highly aware of the time constraints under which teachers have to work, and will know well the merits of 'not reinventing the wheel', to use this overstretched phrase. Therefore encouraging trainees to scrutinise materials to see whether they might be *amended, adapted, refined or updated* is both sensible and supportive. All trainees will be required to demonstrate that they can devise original materials (and many will derive great professional satisfaction from doing so). In reality, however, using one's creative powers to produce original items ought to be paralleled by the deployment of judgement to select materials which, even if less than ideal in their present form, can be made to mesh with the needs of particular learner groups.

Where there is a group of trainees based in an institution, it could be productive to elicit what support there might be for a learning materials 'exhibition'. At such an event, trainees could, in turn, display and describe an aid which they are using, reviewing the ways in which it might be claimed to be enhancing student learning. The rationale for opting for a particular format (e.g. a set of 'Powerpoint' slides rather than a printed handout) can be provided, and pointers provided as to how the aid might be supplemented or further developed. What tends to emerge in such a forum is that trainees from other specialisms (often prompted by the right kind of questioning from a skilled facilitator) discern how the value of particular aids is frequently not exclusive to one specialist domain – with the kind of adaptation and refinement proposed above they will often be seen to be useful more widely.

Awareness of employment-related issues

A sometimes overlooked dimension of mentoring is the value of keeping up to date with what kinds of requirements are being expressed by the PCET sector regarding candidates for teaching posts. I am not implying in what follows that mentors should aspire to become careers advisers, but being able to transmit to trainees 'really useful knowledge' about the realities of employment in the sector is often much appreciated. Of course, trainees can research for themselves what kinds of skills and experience are being sought (by using college websites and simply sending for applicant packs/ post descriptions when jobs are advertised). Where mentors can offer something over and above this resides in their being able to *facilitate the gaining of appropriate experience*. This dimension of the experiential learning being designed for a trainee is one which perhaps focuses on a broader range of dispositions and competences than those exclusively associated with classroom teaching.

To illustrate what is meant, it is evident that employers are increasingly being explicit regarding such things as:

- the ability to write reports to a good standard of literacy;
- being able to provide consultation for students, their parents and other parties;
- personal tutorial responsibilities;
- teamworking;
- being up to date with policy and curriculum developments;
- professional standards in the area of attendance and timekeeping.

While it would probably be unnecessary to point out what exactly mentors should do regarding each of these in turn (and a much longer list would be possible – that above is merely a sample based on what just one sixth form college was recently highlighting) one or two indications might be of value. Regarding *tutoring*, for example, mentors might allow access at least to their own group tutorial sessions, so that the operation of a tutorial curriculum might be observed at first hand. And providing that consent was given by the learner, some individual tutorial work might be sat in on, for instance where a progress review were being conducted. Many trainees (certainly this holds true for those on pre-service courses) will not be given a tutorial role; to an extent this fact can disadvantage them when seeking first posts. Any opportunity to observe what this crucial part of professional activity in PCET entails will be worthwhile. Similarly, facilitating and strongly encouraging attendance at – and, even better, participation by – trainees at 'open evenings' and other such events is sensible. At these, parents and prospective students are given advice as to what the options might be within an institution, and witnessing this process is to be highly recommended. Trainees benefit not only from seeing this at work, but from exposure to an even more diverse mix of individuals than those in their classes.

These kinds of things broaden trainees' understanding of the *raison d'être* of the sector, and will undoubtedly allow them to construct more convincing CVs when applying for posts. In some senses, what mentors can accomplish here on behalf of their trainees has as much to commend it as being able to volunteer to do things such as read drafts of supporting statements and/or provide references in connection with applications.

One important dimension of the current employment scene which mentors may perhaps not have an overview of is the importance being attached to such matters as *reliability* – indeed from the numerous reference requests I have received over the years it almost seems appropriate to describe employability as hinging on 'reliability, reliability, reliability'. Employer requests to specify exact percentages of actual/possible attendances by a trainee are not uncommon, and the same kind of thing applies to punctuality. Mentors would be doing trainees a disservice by not raising their awareness of such realities.

Ultimately, even though the kinds of commitments mentors would offer in these areas are unlikely to be specified as *entitlements* for trainees, they can play an extremely useful part in the socialisation process often viewed as an important strand within mentoring relationships. Self-awareness on mentors' parts regarding what *they themselves* feel they would have liked to be 'taught' (as opposed to having simply 'caught') early on in their careers can play as useful a role in informing what 'non-classroom' opportunities are set up for trainees as keeping abreast of what colleges are seeking in new entrants.

'What do mentors probably not need to do?'

It is perhaps surprising to find the inclusion in this guide of a section with this title. However, there are in fact a number of components of an initial teacher training programme for which clear responsibility rests with trainers/tutors rather than mentors. There is a rational division of labour which is required for the successful delivery of such programmes because (remembering the short time period involved) no single individual can cover every essential. Trainers – often but not exclusively based in universities – are best placed to deal with certain things, while practising college-based subject specialists are without any doubt at all the right people to lead trainees' professional learning relating to other aspects of beginning to teach – some obvious examples being the content knowledge of specialisms, relevant exam board specifications and procedures, and the local facilities – and sometimes constraints – impacting on learning and teaching.

It is entirely legitimate that mentors hold certain expectations regarding what their trainees should know and can do on the basis of their attending an endorsed PCET training course. Were this not to hold true, mentors would simply be overwhelmed by the quantity of information and the nature of some of the principles and concepts they might be expected to impart to trainees. (Which is *not* to imply that mentors would in any way be intellectually challenged by much of the generic material covered by trainers.) There are certainly issues over the greater, more convenient, accessibility for trainers of certain learning and teaching related resources and the availability to universities of speakers who are experts in various policy or practice domains. But the point being made here primarily relates to volume – the sheer quantity of material to be covered is the issue, not any question marks over whether any of it would be beyond the average mentor's range.

To allow for a more efficient concentration of their time and energies, mentors in general would probably be advised not to attempt to deal – at least not on a 'from square one' basis – with such areas as:

- the *basics* of lesson planning (the nature of aims/objectives/outcomes; the need to provide timings for lesson segments; the need to demonstrate variety of learner activities, etc.);
- a *general* review of the principal learning resources available to teachers (the various boards; video; web-based materials, etc.);
- trying to encapsulate the major features of the present landscape of educational policy, or the funding of PCET institutions – trainees do need to acquire a critical understanding of the place of the post-compulsory sector within the wider context of educational provision, current national and international policy shifts and sources of funding but such areas are in general thoroughly reviewed in the training institutions;
- the continuing debates, and disagreements, over inclusivity, personalisation and learning styles, which are being given some prominence on virtually all training programmes.

These are the kinds of 'policy and principles' areas that any self-respecting training programme ought to have perfectly adequately addressed. Some may well need over time to be at least touched on by mentors, but there is no great profit in starting from an assumption of nil knowledge, and nor is there the time which would be needed to do so. Clearly whether or not a trainee has encountered a particular issue, or topic, will depend on the stage they are at on their training programme. (One supplement to the kind of mentors' 'toolkit' proposed in this guide could be a copy of the training institution's taught programme, or its associated module guides, so that it can be ascertained whether something has or has not been dealt with.)

The kind of listing shown above can only ever exemplify what the individual trainee's experience has been. Notwithstanding the ostensibly largely standardised nature of accredited training programmes, certain variations do exist – but these are usually more ones of emphasis rather than of actual content. For this reason there is value in at least looking at what is contained in the trainee's particular course handbook. The mentor's prime role in connection with the kinds of practical/policy issues being addressed by trainers becomes one of facilitating a set of *connections* between these and the local circumstances and opportunities trainees will encounter in a specific institution.

For example, in connection with such crucially important recent legislation as the Single Equality Act (2010), what will be of special relevance for trainees are the set of responses which have been made to this. How has the college refined its selection procedures (for both students and staff) in line with the Act, for example? What physical adaptations to the premises have had to be made? Have any significant adjustments been made to support and guidance structures – and, most importantly, from a trainee's perspective – to the kinds of pedagogies being promoted in the college?

With regard to developments connected to the 14–19 agenda, the sorts of questions that might be addressed were perhaps hinted at by Ruth Silver in one of the numerous articles which collectively formed a kind of 'inquest' on the failure of the Tomlinson Committee Report to achieve all its aims. Her view was that a 14–19 solution will comprise far more than 'beefing up existing collaborative initiatives such as the government's "increased flexibility" programme, under which 14-year-olds disaffected at school can spend a day a week in colleges pursuing more vocational activities':

> There are currently about 100,000 school pupils studying in further education. The future won't simply be more of the same … If we really want 14 to 19 reform, that won't be enough.

> (Silver, in Kingston, 2005)

What a mentor might be raising a trainee's awareness of is, therefore, the current scale of 14–19 provision within the particular institution, how successful it is deemed to have been, and what plans are emerging to refine what is on offer in the light of concerns such as those illustrated above, and the inception of 14–19 Diplomas. The example of 14–19 developments is actually chosen here because, in my experience, the whole debate is one which does appear to unsettle a number of trainees, for reasons hinted at in the same article:

> But wouldn't the wholesale migration of 14-year olds into the essentially adult atmosphere of colleges pose too many problems? 'Full-time 14-year olds in colleges bring all sorts of legal implications of in loco parentis and child protection', says Norman Lucas, director of post-compulsory teacher education at London University's Institute of Education. 'Then you've got the "kiddification" of FE. If you've got hordes of 14-year-olds full-time, the implication is the opposite of the open atmosphere you want for adult education.'

> (ibid.)

The high value of mentors' work here lies, as I have indicated, in filling in all the *local details* of a national picture which have been given the 'broad brush' treatment by a training institution, as it will have been in much of the contemporary literature. What is entailed is clearly having an informed grasp of what is taking place outside of the confines of a specific curriculum department, at different scales and organisational levels within an institution. It may be that one component of such awareness raising as I have advocated will be liaising with key personnel to obtain from them relevant materials – and possibly even agreement to talk informally with a trainee regarding 'work in progress' within an institution to meet the requirements of emerging national policy for the PCET sector.

References

Anderson, E. M., and Lucasse Shannon, A. (1995) Towards a conceptualisation of mentoring, in T. Kerry and A. Shelton Mayes (eds), *Issues in Mentoring*, London: Routledge.

Ball, S. (2008) Performativity, privatisation, professionals and the state, in B. Cunningham (ed.), *Exploring Professionalism,* London: Bedford Way Papers

Cardiff University (2003) *Teaching Practice Guide for Students, Mentors and Link Tutors*, Cardiff: School of Social Sciences, Cardiff University.

Colley, H. (2003) *Mentoring for Social Inclusion: A Critical Approach to Nurturing Mentor Relationships*, London: RoutledgeFalmer.

Cunningham, B. (2000) Beginning close encounters: on starting to teach in colleges, *Teacher Development*, 4/3: 241–56.

DfES (2004) *Equipping our Teachers for the Future: Reforming Initial Teacher Training for the Learning and Skills Sector*, Nottingham: Department for Education and Skills.

FENTO (2001) *Mentoring Towards Excellence*, London: Further Education National Training Organisation.

Fry, H., Ketteridge, S., and Marshall, S. (1999) *A Handbook for Teaching and Learning in Higher Education: Enhancing Academic Practice*, London: Kogan Page.

Goleman, D. (1999) *Working with Emotional Intelligence*, London: Bloomsbury.

Guile, D., and Lucas, N. (1999) Rethinking initial teacher education and professional development in further education: towards the learning professional, in A. Green and N. Lucas (eds), *FE and Lifelong Learning: Realigning the Sector for the Twenty-First Century,* London: Bedford Way Papers.

Hargreaves, A., and Fullan, M. G. (1992) *Understanding Teacher Development*, New York: Teachers College Press.

Healy, C. C., and Welchert, A. J. (1990) Mentoring relations: a definition to advance research and practice, *Educational Researcher*, 19/9: 17–21.

Hoyle, E. (1974) Professionality, professionalism and control in teaching, *London Educational Review*, 3/2: 13–19

Huberman, M. (1992) Teacher development and instructional mastery, in A. Hargreaves and M. G. Fullan (eds), *Understanding Teacher Development*, New York: Teachers College Press.

Huddleston, P., and Unwin, L. (2007) *Teaching and Learning in Further Education,* (3rd edn), London: RoutledgeFalmer.

Jackson, P. W. (1992) Helping teachers develop, in A. Hargreaves and M. G. Fullan (eds), *Understanding Teacher Development*, New York: Teachers College Press.

Johnson, W. B., and Ridley, C. R. (2004) *The Elements of Mentoring*, New York: Palgrave Macmillan.

Kingston, P. (2004) More colleges fail in south, *Education Guardian*, 30 November.

Kingston, P. (2005) Opportunity knocks, *Guardian*, 22 February.

Napper, R., and Batchelor, D. (1989) *A Tutor's Toolkit: An Open Learning Resource for First Time Tutors*, Cambridge: National Extension College.

Pask, R., and Joy, B. (2007) *Mentoring-Coaching: A Handbook for Education Professionals*, Buckingham: Open University Press.

Sachs, J. (2003) Teacher professional identity: competing discourses, competing outcomes, *Journal of Education Policy*, 16/2: 149–61.

University of East London (2010) *Cass School of Education, Programme Handbook, PGCE (PCET), 2010–2011*, London: University of East London.

Waterhouse, P. (1991) *Tutoring*, Stafford: Network Educational.

Mentoring and models of professional learning

■ to enable mentors to confidently underpin their practice by being able to draw on selected models of professional learning.

How feasible are the aspirations of those who hope to codify teachers' craft knowledge? It is not difficult to find maxims or practical tips to pass on to beginning teachers, but what do they all add up to? … Can an amorphous collection of practical principles be said to constitute a grounded theory of practice, or is this mere wishful thinking?

(Michael Eraut, 1994)

Practice without a grounding of theory is likely to be sterile at best, and ineffective and damaging at worst. Being sent straight into the classroom for a large block of time without a chance of reflection is not the best way.

(From letter titled 'Real teacher training',
Education Guardian, 22 March 2005)

It is hoped that at least some exposure to what will be a relatively limited range of theory (in the form of selected models of professionalism and professional learning) will add both interest and insight to the activity of mentoring. As with all professional work worthy of the description, mentoring is not merely concerned with practicalities and a mechanistic, rule-bound, approach to tasks. Some cognisance of broader, conceptual, frameworks which might underpin the activity is very worthwhile, if not actually essential. To this end I will therefore select a small number of theoretical perspectives that it appears can profitably *be applied* to the process of understanding the contribution which effective mentoring might make to the early professional development of PCET teachers.

It needs to be stressed, however, that the models are only being presented in skeletal form, and that none are derived specifically from research in our sector.

A possibly extreme example of what I am describing is that, while we may well find 'transferable', valuable and illuminating a construct such as Vygotsky's 'zone of proximal development' (ZPD) – and its seminal depiction of the role of 'more knowledgeable others' – it was actually derived from an exploration of learning in early childhood (Wells, 1999).

In their 1995 paper on the training of college teachers, Michael Young *et al.* referred to the 'benign neglect' that they saw as having long afflicted the post-compulsory sector. One of the ways in which this was in fact evident was to be found in a real dearth of literature devoted to professional issues in the PCET sector. This observation is one contrasting strongly with what has long been available with a focus on school teaching. To a large extent, not a great deal has changed over the past fifteen years or so: a high proportion of what is published on *professional* – as opposed to *policy* – issues still originates in work focused on phases of education other than PCET. It is for this reason that the reader will find so little here based on researching college teachers. And certain of the perspectives apply more strongly to 'learning *teaching*' than 'learning *mentoring*' but, as I hope will be evident, trying to draw a border between these two types of professional learning may in fact be neither straightforward nor productive.

'Artisanry' and the learning of a craft

To begin this chapter, the notion of teaching as a craft skill is an interesting one, which has been particularly thoughtfully examined by Michael Huberman. Although his exposition of the 'craft' model makes no explicit reference to mentoring, we can see without too much difficulty where a skilled mentor could play a crucial role:

> Essentially, teachers are artisans [and it is useful to reflect on the significance of the 'art' here, I would claim], primarily working alone, with a variety of new and cobbled together materials, in a personally designed work environment. They gradually develop a repertoire of instructional skills and strategies, corresponding to a progressively denser, more differentiated and well-integrated set of mental schemata: they come to read the instructional situation better and faster, and to respond to it with a greater variety of tools. They develop this repertoire through a somewhat haphazard process of trial and error, usually when one or another segment of the repertoire does not work repeatedly. Somewhere in that cycle *they may reach out to peers or … professional trainers* [and] transform those inputs into a more private, personally congenial form.
>
> (Huberman, 1992: 136; emphasis added)

For 'peers or … professional trainers' I would claim it would now be entirely legitimate to substitute 'mentors'; after all, in the specific US educational context Huberman had in mind (certainly at the time he was observing its key features) the role of formal mentors would have been minuscule. The point which can surely be emphasised is that mentoring allows for far more *active* interventions than are alluded to above, where inputs are obtained purely on the basis of a 'reaching out' by someone in the process of developing their craft skills. Effective mentors can potentially initiate an *acceleration* of trainees' professional learning in a context where they are not simply passive, until such a time as they are reached out to. This is not to negate the significance of trial and error learning. The importance of this has been drawn attention to by other writers, such as David Hargreaves (1999); mentors' regular inputs will productively complement this, not replace it. They will, by encouraging open discussion of the 'errors' – the things which '[do] not work repeatedly' – deepen trainees' understanding of these, and can engage in reviewing possible alternative strategies – or 'tools' in Huberman's phrasing.

What will be an essential precondition for the above formulation to be a credible one will obviously be the degree to which a mentor (and/or a department) has explicitly allowed a trainee 'the freedom to fail'. This hinges on the key question of whether a trainee will be fearful of the consequences of owning up to mistakes – or will feel secure and comfortable in doing so. As one trainee put it: 'Making us feel that no mistake is disastrous would be great'. (FT, pre-service trainee, 2004). But such a consideration applies, of course, to many of the models relating to professional learning, and certainly to most of those which will comprise the rest of the present brief review.

Learning through reflection on experience

Experiential learning is probably the one single theoretical perspective likely to be of special utility to mentors. The term is perhaps most frequently associated with the work of Kolb (1984) although there are a number of other writers – both before and after Kolb – who examine the key dimensions of learning from experience. Dennison and Kirk (1990), for example, adopting the brilliantly succinct formula 'Do, Review, Learn, Apply' (and using this for the title of their important book), look at the process in a particularly accessible way.

Experiential learning, we might argue, forms the core of what teacher training is 'all about'. Yes, trainees are inducted into a broad policy context for post-compulsory education, they are taught how to draft lesson plans, prepare stimulating learning materials and so on. But at the very heart of their professional learning, and their preparation for a career in teaching, lie the realities of the classroom. Coping with these realities, responding to the challenges they pose and effectively managing student learning within the constraints presented by them, can all be enhanced by *mentors' skills in facilitating experiential learning*.

For a trainee, this type of learning will almost certainly comprise such elements as reflecting upon and evaluating his or her own performance, involving being able to evaluate one's own *current* practice, and plan for *future* practice, ideally thinking especially about how engaging in continuing professional development might best promote further improvement.

If there is one set of constructs that the great majority of mentors will already have encountered it is almost certain that it concerns *reflection*. The idea of 'the reflective practitioner' (Schön, 1983) permeates virtually all initial teacher training programmes, and has done for some time now – certainly since the early 1990s. This means that many mentors will themselves, therefore, have encountered it, in one version or another, in their own training. My intention now, however, is to look at ways of applying the ideas of reflective practice – and experiential learning as it is so strongly related as a model – to mentoring as a strategy for enhancing professional learning. Given the claims being made for the centrality of experiential learning, what ought we to understand of its essentials?

A number of names are associated with what is now a very significant body of work examining the links between experience, learning and personal or professional development. The boundaries between the perspectives which these writers have, in turn, presented are sometimes rather blurred ones. It would be unprofessional to contend that any one model simply 'recycles' the contents of an earlier one, though, as each does have its own distinctive interpretation of the processes involved in reflecting on experience, learning from this and 'moving on'. The significance attached to a cyclical dimension of such a set of actions is far greater in certain models (especially, say, Kolb, 1984) than others (notably Schön's formulation). The similarities and overlapping territory are, however, evident.

Interestingly what it was which originally struck Donald Schön, and which led him to the focus of his seminal work (*The Reflective Practitioner: How Professionals Think in Action*), was that in his view universities' particular view of knowledge 'fosters selective inattention to practical competence and professional artisanry' (Schön, 1983: p. vii). He examines a number of what he called 'vignettes of practice' drawn from fields such as architecture and engineering, concentrating in particular 'on episodes in which a senior practitioner tries to help a junior one learn to do something' (ibid., p. viii). It is not that easy – or legitimate – to attempt to encapsulate all of Schön's ideas which he illustrates by use of his 'vignettes' but it is certainly worth drawing attention to one of his most significant contentions. This is that many professionals, to paraphrase, are at risk of becoming locked into a mode of practice where their technical expertise and rationality *is not interrogated*. Their knowledge of why they act in certain ways (e.g. when dealing with a client) remains *tacit*, and they 'find nothing in the world of practice to occasion reflection' (Schön, 1983: 69). This fact limits both their ability to deal with novel ('surprising' is the word Schön uses) situations, and to communicate with others what has been informing their approach to a particular 'case', beyond restating certain relevant 'technical' principles that they have tended to base their actions on.

For practitioners such as Schön is alluding to here, 'uncertainty is a threat; its admission a sign of weakness' (ibid.). What is proposed in *The Reflective Practitioner*, one of its central contentions, is that professional behaviour will become more insightful, responsive to the novelty of 'cases' *and* susceptible to clear articulation to other professionals if the merits of what the author described as *reflection-in-action* were to be acknowledged and its use to become 'broader, deeper, and more rigorous' (ibid.). Reflection-in-action promotes an open enquiry into the *why* of professional acts alongside the simple description of what form these acts have taken. It is true that some practitioners are acknowledged by Schön to already engage in reflection-in-action, but what he argues for is that it should become 'a dominant pattern of practice' (ibid., p. 354). In our present context, that of mentoring, the reciprocal benefits that are likely to accrue from this development are ones that are, I hope, quite evident.

An especially accessible version of the central tenets of experiential learning is to be found in Bill Dennison and Roger Kirk's *Do, Review, Learn, Apply* (1990). These authors are primarily concerned with how teachers may create and manage opportunities for experiential learning in learner groups. It is therefore concerned with the teacher–student relationship. However, what is interesting about Dennison and Kirk's framework is that it is so eminently transferable from the original context to that of mentoring activities. For example, the authors try to steer teachers away from a didactic, transmission-based style and towards one in which their principal strategy becomes *organising opportunities* for learners to move through the cycle of learning begun by *doing* (the 'concrete experience' of Kolb's formulation). They, furthermore, put forward a notion that it is possible to set up successive cycles, from each of which something of significance is learnt. The incremental nature of learning is thus neatly underscored, but more importantly the confidence-building nature of the process is emphasised:

> Perceptions about success attract students towards more learning cycles ... there is no more effective means of boosting confidence and raising enthusiasm than the successful completion of a learning cycle.
>
> (Dennison and Kirk, 1990: 20–1)

The authors convincingly relate their 'Do, Review, Learn, Apply' (DRLA) model to Kolb's idea of a learning cycle, as shown in Figure 3.1.

I do not believe it is at all tenuous to maintain that what was originally being proposed as a device for enhancing student learning also has much to offer mentors planning how to structure *the professional learning of their trainees*. The DRLA model can be successfully adopted as part of the mentoring repertoire by:

■ organising experiences which will represent an appropriate level of challenge (e.g. a particular class to teach; a stipulation that a particular learning resource is incorporated into a session);

■ providing ample opportunities to discuss the professional learning deriving from the experience (especially in the context of post-observation debriefing);

■ encouraging trainees to record their reflections on the experience and, especially, to identify ways in which any generalisable principles seem to emerge from the experience (this stage can be worked through using the self-evaluation section of teaching observation proformas which is almost always now provided, and/or in trainees' reflective logs);

■ negotiating with trainees how they will implement whatever refinements to their professional practice which, having been around the cycle, they now see as being worthwhile.

What is of real value here is the role of the mentor in using DRLA to assist a trainee to move out of their 'comfort zone'. Trainees, in being stimulated to review how things might be better/could be refined, will thus be focusing on what they will do differently; they will not have the safety and comfort of knowing for certain

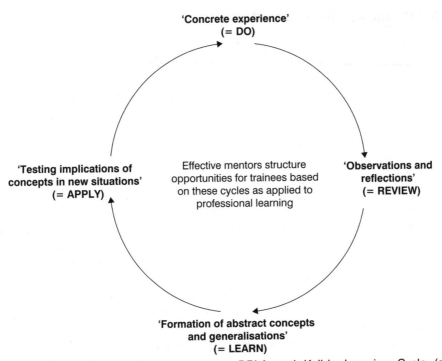

'Concrete experience'
(= DO)

'Testing implications of
concepts in new situations'
(= APPLY)

Effective mentors structure
opportunities for trainees based
on these cycles as applied to
professional learning

'Observations and
reflections'
(= REVIEW)

'Formation of abstract concepts
and generalisations'
(= LEARN)

FIGURE 3.1 The relationship between DRLA and Kolb's Learning Cycle (after Dennison and Kirk, 1990: 18)

that a change in strategy will achieve better results, but at least they will try such a change rather than simply opting for a repetition of what they have done before. Their learning will have been, in the Brunerian sense, adequately *scaffolded* (Bruner, 1960).

As noted later on in this guide, reflective practice has not been without its detractors. One criticism it might be worth mentioning at this stage, given the claims I make for being able to link critical reflection with consequential action is that of Cornford, who believes a:

> weakness inherent in many reflective paradigms is the failure to take account of a long recognised problem in human learning – forgetting. Simply being critical is not enough to guarantee that those critical thoughts will be remembered or that those thoughts can be translated into effective procedural action.
>
> (Cornford, 2002: 228)

Perhaps the message for mentors embodied in this particular view is that they will need to *revisit* significant matters, over a period of time – in much the same way as we build reviews of student learning into our designs for covering any syllabus with a group. This is to advocate no more nor less than working to a 'spiral syllabus' model (Bruner, 1960) rather than one where topics, once covered, are only encountered again at the summative assessment stage.

'Co-constructing' professional learning

A model that views effective professional learning as being especially contingent on dialogue invokes the notion of 'co-construction'. This is conceptualised as a process distinct from *instructional* models of learning, or *constructional;* the most supportive and empowering mentors are particularly unlikely to opt for instructional approaches, given that these are ones focusing more on teaching rather than learning, and are based on a noted power imbalance in the mentoring relationship. Rogers (2004) and others such as Carnell *et al.* (2006) have argued that such features tend to make for ultimately unproductive mentoring.

Adopting a co-construction perspective on professional learning essentially draws on a model where *dialogue* is of central concern in reaching a joint understanding. The nature of the 'learning-centred conversations' illustrated by Carnell *et al.* (2006: 30–1) reveals that it is strongly related to the DRLA cycle I have outlined above. Among the positive attributes of such learning through dialogue are, for example, its 'focus on social and collaborative approaches' and the way in which it 'value[s] processes which enhance collaborative *outcomes*' (ibid., p. 6; emphasis added). In drawing special attention to the outcomes that are potentially engendered by co-construction, I am, incidentally but importantly, pointing to the ways in which dialogue deepens the understandings of both trainee and mentor – a mutuality I return to in Chapter 5, when highlighting some of the rewards of mentoring.

'Stages' and mentoring

There appears to be a fundamental connection between the stage of professional development a trainee is at and the nature (or stage) of the mentoring which will be most appropriate. One possibly useful theoretical construct which can be drawn on to illustrate this proposition is that of the 'dichotomies' which Dubin (1961) believed it was possible to identify, and on which a number of other writers have subsequently elaborated. A summary version of the dichotomies is shown as Figure 3.2.

At the core of Dubin's model are contrasts relating to self-knowledge; no particular claims were made for the applicability of the ideas to the specifics of mentoring, but nevertheless such an application does seem entirely valid. some diagrammatic representations of the dichotomies show them ascending a 'staircase', i.e. with UI (unconscious incompetence) on the lowest step and UC (unconscious competence) on the highest; this may in fact be the form in which the model is most accessible to mentors.

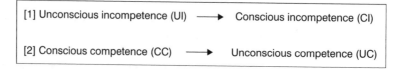

FIGURE 3.2 From unconscious incompetence to unconscious competence, after Dubin, 1961.

In the mentoring context, what we can conceive of is a scenario where, initially, a trainee makes mistakes (= is incompetent) *because they do not appreciate how or why they are such*. This, earliest, stage of their starting to teach is, then, when they are unconsciously incompetent, and – from the mentor's perspective – especially merit a tolerant and patient approach. More importantly, what they also need, to allow them to move to the stage of '*conscious* incompetence', is an opportunity to discuss why whatever it is they have done is not good practice; the reasons will generally emerge through a skilfully managed discussion, although ultimately mentors may need to recourse to a measure of exposition to allow these to surface.

Once a trainee appreciates the need to refine their practice in a particular regard, the mentor will then suggest (and facilitate if need be) further opportunities for them to experiment. The trainee at this stage will be, more often than not, highly self-conscious (especially if being observed) but – it is hoped – 'getting it right', rather than repeating their earlier mistakes. This stage would accord with Dubin's notion of *conscious competence* – or a state which some observers of teaching have compared with the careful, 'by the book', road skills of many newly licensed drivers; they are (or so it is said) highly aware of all their actions in operating the controls of the car, keeping to speed limits and responding to other road users and so on.

The mentor's role at this conscious competence stage would be to comment on the infringement of any best practice guidelines which had been discussed with a trainee. Having raised the trainee's consciousness concerning particular facets of flawed classroom practice they consequently need feel somewhat less hesitant in offering their criticism.

To pursue the analogy with learning to drive, for the teacher, as with the driver, a stage comes in their experience when, to a greater or lesser extent, they perform on the basis of 'second nature'. Obviously we have now arrived at the *unconscious competence* stage, where we do not have to 'stop to think' about every single classroom action.

It is, though, only appropriate to point out here that a 'dichotomies' framework may have certain serious limitations within the kind of time span which we know teacher training occupies (see Introduction). It could well be that there is simply insufficient developmental time available to trainees for them to arrive at the 'unconscious competence' stage, and that this will only be a feature of their later professional development – perhaps of Huberman's 'stabilisation' phase, which he felt dawned only after four to six years of classroom experience (Huberman, 1992: 127).

On the other hand, some mentors – and, more broadly, educationalists – may feel that teachers should never become so unselfconscious that they stop fairly constant self-monitoring their performance. They may become *more conscious of their learner groups than of themselves*, using their 'antennae' to pick up how successfully a lesson is turning out (and modifying its pitch and pace in line with the 'signals' they are receiving). But they never totally lose a measure of self-awareness, and a consciousness of why they are teaching using a certain strategy or mix of strategies.

The Dreyfus model of skills acquisition is an interesting, much-cited, one which also hinges on the notion of 'stages', a few aspects of each I indicate below, with professional skills developing through the following stages:

- Level 1 *Novice* (where, for example, there will be a 'rigid adherence to taught rules or plans')
- Level 2 *Advanced Beginner* (here, 'situational perception' is still limited)
- Level 3 *Competent* (an interesting feature of this stage being 'coping with crowdedness')
- Level 4 *Proficient* (where 'decision-making is less laboured')
- Level 5 *Expert* (by which stage there exists not only an 'intuitive grasp of situations based on tacit understanding' but a 'vision of what is possible').

(Dreyfus and Dreyfus, 1986)

Mentors will, in general, be working with individuals progressing through levels 1 to 3, but some trainees may of course display skills development beyond these stages by the end of their programmes – while, out of modesty, some mentors might not claim to have arrived at the 'Expert' stage.

A number of authors have given special prominence to far more explicit notions of actual *mentoring* 'life cycles' or 'stages', seeing these as fundamental to our knowledge of how mentoring works. Healy and Welchert touch on this idea, dealing, for example, with the issue of what may happen at 'the separation juncture' when both parties must 'either redefine their relationship based on collegiality or suffer a deteriorating alliance' (Healy and Welchert, 1990: 20): this question can be seen to have special resonance in situations where the trainee has also been a colleague training on an in-service basis.

However, fuller treatments of the ideas about the stages which mentoring relationships go through can probably be found in such forays into this area as those of Kram (1983) This is a more complex approach than can be readily summarised here, but a most succinct perspective on the concept of 'stages' which is worth mentioning is that promoted by the Centre for Excellence in Leadership (CEL, 2004). This simple model (derived from Alred *et al.*, 1998) sees the mentoring process which best facilitates learning and development as moving through only three stages, as in Figure 3.3.

This may appear to oversimplify what is entailed in mentoring processes, discounting for example the possibility of the rejection by mentees[1] of ideas which they may have been encouraged to 'explore'. However, it seems to serve quite well as the kind of basic framework which could be presented to trainees as an accessible explanation of 'what mentoring is all about'.

Some concluding thoughts

Although some practitioners may well continue to have reservations concerning the utility of theory (and some may even have tended to decry it), I hope to have been able in this chapter to render accessible some theoretical work that I believe may helpfully inform mentoring practice. In a policy environment where post-compulsory education has in much the same way as schools been subject to what Hoyle (1982) termed a 'turn to the practical', theory may bestow on us, in Ball's phrasing, a tool for 'thinking otherwise': 'it offers a language for challenge and modes of thought, other than those articulated for us by dominant others' (1995: 266). An engagement with theory can enhance our capacity to move beyond what Freidson (1994) called a 'commonsense' idea of professionalism.

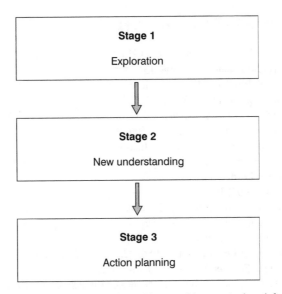

FIGURE 3.3 One possible interpretation of 'stages' in mentoring (after CEL, 2004)

The ability and confidence to employ theoretical perspectives in our work, and in our reflections on professional expertise, may thus be viewed as fundamentally empowering. Michael Eraut has written that 'the most important quality of the professional teacher [is] the disposition to theorise' and expressed the view that:

> If our students acquire and sustain this disposition they will go on developing their theorising capacities throughout their teaching careers, they will be genuinely self-evaluative and they will continue to search for, invent and implement new ideas. Without it they will become prisoners of their early ... experience, perhaps the competent teachers of today, almost certainly the ossified teachers of tomorrow.
>
> (Eraut, 1994: 71)

Teachers according to Sachs are confronted by such a range of challenges that they:

> need to be skilled practitioners who can work both collaboratively and independently; have *the ability to solve complex practical and theoretical problems*; are able to reflect on their practice in order to develop quality learning opportunities for their students and are professionals who are able to cope with rapid social and technological change.
>
> (1997: 263–4; emphasis added)

If there does exist such an entity as a 'theory–practice gap', i.e. one between the academic approach and language of the university and the practical concerns and challenges being faced every day in post-compulsory education, then no one appears better placed to bridge this gap than a mentor with well-honed 'interpretive' skills.

References

Alred, G., Garvey, B. and Smith, R. (1998) Pas de deux – learning in conversation, *Career Development International*, 3/7: 308–13.

Ball, S. J. (1995) Intellectuals or technicians: the urgent role of theory in educational studies, *British Journal of Educational Studies*, 43/2: 255–71.

Bruner, J. (1960) *The Process of Education*, Cambridge, MA: Harvard University Press.

Carnell, E., MacDonald. J. and Askew, S. (2006) *Coaching and Mentoring in Higher Education: A Learning-Centred Approach*, London: Institute of Education, University of London.

CEL (2004) *Mentoring: Learning from Practice, Learning from Each Other*, London: Centre for Excellence in Leadership.

Cornford, I. R. (2002) Reflective teaching: empirical research findings and some implications for teacher education, *Journal of Vocational Education and Training* 54/2: 219–35.

Dennison, B., and Kirk, R. (1990) *Do, Review, Learn, Apply: A Simple Guide to Experiential Learning*, Oxford: Blackwell.

Dreyfus, H. L., and Dreyfus, S.E. (1986) *Mind over Machine: The Power of Human Intuition and Expertise in the Era of the Computer*, Oxford: Blackwell.

Dubin, R. (1961) *Human Relations in Administration with Readings and Cases*, Englewood Cliffs, NJ: Prentice-Hall.

Eraut, M. (1994) *Developing Professional Knowledge and Competence*, London: Falmer Press.

FENTO (2000) *Standards for Teaching and Supporting Learning in Further Education in England and Wales*, London: Further Education National Training Organisation.

Freidson, E. (1994) *Professionalism Reborn: Theory, Prophecy and Policy*, Chicago, IL: University of Chicago Press.

Hargreaves, D. (1999) 'Ask the Experts', *Times Educational Supplement*, 12 February.

Healy, C. C., and Welchert, A. J. (1990) Mentoring relations: a definition to advance research and practice. *Educational Researcher*, 19/9: 17–21.

Hoyle, E. (1982) The professionalism of teachers: a paradox, *British Journal of Educational Studies*, 30/2: 161–71.

Huberman, M. (1992) Teacher development and instructional mastery, in A. Hargreaves and M. G. Fullan (eds) *Understanding Teacher Development*, New York: Teachers College Press.

Kolb, D. A. (1984) *Experiential Learning: Experience as the Source of Learning and Development*, Englewood Cliffs, NJ: Prentice-Hall.

Kram, K. E. (1983) Phases of the mentor relationship, *Academy of Management Journal*, 26/4: 608–25.

Rogers, J. (2004) *Coaching Skills: A Handbook*, Milton Keynes: Open University Press.

Sachs, J. (1997) Reclaiming the agenda of teacher professionalism: an Australian experience, *Journal of Education for Teaching*, 23/3: 263–75.

Schön, D. (1983) *The Reflective Practitioner: How Professionals Think in Action* (2nd edn 1991), Aldershot: Arena.

Wells, G. (1999) *Dialogic Inquiries in Education: Building on the Legacy of Vygotsky*, Cambridge: Cambridge University Press.

Young, M., Lucas, N., Sharp, G. and Cunningham, B. (1995) *Teacher Training for the FE Sector: Training the Lecturer of the Future*, London: Post-16 Education Centre, Institute of Education, University of London.

4

Observing classroom teaching

Chapter objectives

- to outline the rationale for observations, illustrate best practice, and provide certain important cautions relating to this activity.

> T4: With Michael Cohen observing. I have never seen those tough nuts being coy before! I wonder if my own nervousness communicated itself to them.
>
> (Nicholas Otty, *Learner Teacher*)

This particular aspect of mentoring in colleges merits a whole chapter to itself for reasons most of which might appear obvious. In fact even giving the issue this much prominence here does not match the attention it has received with regard to other sectors of education; a fuller treatment of aspects of observation may be found, for example in Ted Wragg's still excellent book focusing on school teaching (Wragg, 1999). Much of the advice this contains is eminently transferable to college contexts.

It is, almost without exception, the single most important challenge facing trainees that they know they will be regularly observed teaching. From long experience as a teacher trainer I would say that the anxieties this aspect of training, and assessment, engenders are greater than that which virtually any other dimension of ITE programmes give rise to. Programme materials typically introduce the issue of observations very supportively:

> The assessment of practical teaching is the area of assessment most likely to cause you anxiety. Even the most experienced of teachers usually feel anxious about their teaching being assessed, so it is hardly surprising that as a trainee this will worry you.
>
> (University of East London, 2010: 33)

With the current framework as specified for the frequency of observations, whether a trainee is enrolled on a full-time or part-time programme it will entail them being observed by tutors/mentors eight times altogether.

Not everyone will necessarily be daunted by the prospect of their teaching being observed, however. Every now and again we encounter trainees who, for example, have already completed short, but intensive, programmes such as ESOL-focused courses, e.g. CELTA,[1] and where observation has traditionally been 'a part of the grammar' of what takes place each week. Frequently video or audio recording of peer teaching may have been included. For someone who has already experienced this kind of approach, there will be far less that is novel or intimidating about having a tutor or mentor in the classroom observing how things are going. The presence of the figure at the back of the room with a clipboard (or, increasingly, a tablet PC) is a far less worrying matter.

In a slightly different vein, there do always seem to be some individuals who are so naturally confident, extroverted or – in some cases – used to 'performing' (former actors, for instance, now undergoing training in the teaching of drama or performing arts) that they are quite unfazed by the prospect of observation. Such trainees are naturally advantaged when it comes to observation, at the very least because they appear able to mask – to their learners as well as their observer – any nervousness they might be experiencing.

From the mentors' perspective, conducting an observation of a trainee is perhaps the best opportunity which will present itself – especially at the debriefing stage – for assisting someone to jump across a gap (or a gulf in some cases) between their present performance and what is desired. Put in extremely simple form diagrammatically (see Figure 4.1), the presence of a mentor on the right side of such a gap can make the crucial difference between trainee's practice evolving or fossilising.

Some essential preliminaries and cautions

Observation of a trainee's class should never take place in any kind of a vacuum. Both parties – observer and observee – need to have, as essential preliminaries, a 'profile' of the learner group being taught, the syllabus they are following and so on. It is, further, essential that a number of issues are addressed before the mentor ever sets foot in the trainee's classroom, and it is such issues with which we are concerned in what follows.

The most sensible starting point is simply reviewing for the person who is going to be observed such things as

- the *rationale* for observation;
- the *status* of the observation to be conducted (i.e. is it *formative* or *summative*?);
- the *format* of the observation;
- the most appropriate '*behaviour*' of the observer.

I shall now deal with each of these in turn.

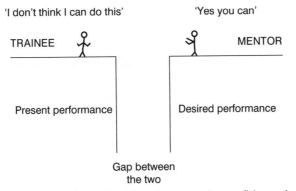

'I don't think I can do this'   'Yes you can'

TRAINEE   MENTOR

Present performance   Desired performance

Gap between
the two

FIGURE 4.1 Improving trainees' performance by confidence-building

Rationale for observation

What is meant here is that the mentor lays out (and this might seem obvious) the reasons why the trainee is going to be observed, the context for observation in the PCET sector generally, and the benefits which it is hoped will come about as a result of the exercise.

Mentors might, for example, draw attention to the fact that, for any 'licence to practise', practical skills have to be assessed alongside theoretical knowledge: no driver, airline pilot or surgeon can be certificated solely on the basis of their grasp of theory, and it is only fitting that this kind of consideration applies equally to new teachers (who certainly have, it could be argued, almost the same potential to cause harm where their professional expertise has not been appropriately tested). The requirements of the specific training provider, and the recommendations of the Inspectorate (OfSTED, 2003) can be cited as well, of course.

Alongside covering such points, the routinisation of classroom observation in the sector can usefully be stressed. As in other phases of education, classrooms can no longer be conceived of as 'secret gardens' in which teachers' interaction with learners is in some ways very much a private, individual, affair with little or no scrutiny being applied to it. In most PCET contexts, being observed has become commonplace and there are real benefits to be gained from trainees becoming acclimatised to this fact at an early stage. Although, as indicated, many people are nervous or hesitant about being observed it is virtually always something about which greater confidence and calmness develop the more often observation is experienced. It is worth spelling this out. Right from the point where trainees apply for first (or subsequent) posts, observation will be a feature of life. Besides its increasing use as part of selection processes (where, in addition to '10 minute presentations', actual lessons taught to real learners are sometimes now required of applicants), observation will be encountered as part of probation, appraisal, peer-review structures and the kinds of internal review used in institutions to ensure their 'inspection-readiness'. And of course the importance of observation within the inspection regime itself can be highlighted.

It is also very worthwhile trying to demonstrate empathy with a trainee by recounting one's own experience of being on the receiving end of observation. Trainees may on occasion not find it that easy to connect with the notion that their observers may themselves have had to be seen working with groups, and might even have experienced 'nerves'.

Overarching all of the above considerations, however, the onus must be on observers to do two things in connection with the process of teaching observation. These are:

1. Negotiating with the person being observed whether there are any particular elements of the teaching session on which feedback would be especially welcome. This gives the trainee a degree of *ownership* of what is going to take place. Towards the end of the series of the required eight observations it may well be that this kind of negotiation has to focus on the kinds of targets agreed following earlier observed sessions, but even in this context the trainee is being given a voice.
2. Stressing the fundamentally *supportive* and *developmental* nature of the process. Teaching observations ought never to be based on a deficit model ('what kind of skills has this person not yet mastered?'). The observer is in the room – in this very specific context – as a mentor-coach, motivated to share as best they can their expertise, and their insights into what constitutes effective learning and teaching. They will certainly have in mind the interests of the learners in the room, workshop, dance studio or whatever other setting the observation is being conducted in, but their principal objective is the enhancement of the trainee's competence and confidence.

Status of observation

Observation takes place for a variety of purposes, and not all of these are susceptible to being ranked as of equal status. For example, initially mentors may suggest to trainees that they sit in on classes on an entirely *informal* basis – perhaps just to 'be on hand' in case any early practical problems arise with which the trainee might value some support. It is important that mentors make quite clear that if things go wrong for trainees on such occasions then nothing is being 'recorded, and might be used as evidence'. The trainee needs to feel that the observer's presence is motivated wholly by positive reasons to do with support, and the opportunity to perhaps provide some initial, friendly, feedback on how first 'close encounters' (Cunningham, 2000) have seemed to them. There is a difference between observations being conducted for *formative* purposes – in reality, half, or over half, of ITE-related observations will fall into this category – and ones where a *summative* statement of some kind (and typically a grading for the observed session) will be the end product.

The status of observations can be, to some degree, negotiable: the trainee's readiness for a formal, recorded, observation should wherever possible be arrived at by taking their own views strongly into account. In situations where a trainee appears especially, but without any real foundation, hesitant regarding formal observation it may, though, be worth using such strongly encouraging, positive, language as 'but you really do seem to me to have settled in, and are confident enough with the group, to do well in a formal observation'.

Format of observation

What this term covers includes such matters as informing trainees whether an *observation proforma* will be used, and for what purpose. If so, it is extremely valuable to discuss what is going to be recorded in the respective sections of any such proforma – this gives the trainee a sense of what will be being looked for. Mentors can say things like 'this part asks me to comment on whether your aids to learning (boardwork, handouts, video clips and so on) were well integrated into the session'.

It is possible, without being guilty of unethical behaviour, for a mentor to even illustrate the kinds of comments that have been made on previous trainees. This should bring into pre-observation discussions a helpful sense of the ways in which any comments on flaws in a lesson have been complemented by constructive suggestions for improvements. Clearly, though, it will be important to ensure that the identity of the previous observee cannot be known as a result of showing a trainee this sort of material. (The most open mentors may feel comfortable in sharing with a trainee the contents of observation reports they have received on *their own* practice. As a strategy for deepening the mentoring relationship this has much to commend it, but of course does carry with it a very special type of risk.)

In connection with the use of observation proformas it is evidently important that a trainee is not kept in the dark about the readership of whatever report is being written. Is it exclusively for the trainee, to inform their own reflections? Is it one to be held only in the mentor's files? Or is it a document that will be read by such figures as a departmental manager, a staff development manager/coordinator, someone with a personnel function and/or a representative of the training provider (most usually a university tutor)?

Also under the heading of the 'format' of the observation we could perhaps consider whether the mentor should be in any significant way a participant in the observed session, but this issue is addressed in connection with aspects of mentor 'behaviour' below.

Observer 'behaviour'

As well as being explicit about whether notes will be being taken, a proforma completed, etc., mentors should negotiate such aspects of the observed session as *how it will be presented to learners*. Does the trainee want to say anything to the learner group to explain the presence of the observer? Should the mentor – especially if the group is one which they themselves have taught, or are currently teaching – take on this role? Or should nothing at all be communicated to the group, in the hope that this will minimise any effects ('observer effects') on learners' behaviour? It is, in reality, all but impossible to ever achieve a state of affairs where a group is entirely unaware of an additional presence in the classroom, so on balance it probably is worth suggesting to a trainee that they say something by way of explanation, even if this only comprises a neutral statement that X is 'visiting the group today'.

It is only considerate to plan on being as unobtrusive as possible in an observed class. Other things being equal, 'back of the room' will always be best for both trainee and learners – less intimidating for the former; less distracting for the latter. But the question 'and where would you prefer me to sit?' is only courteous and considerate.

However, whatever steps an observer might take to minimise a trainee's stress on being observed, sometimes this emotion may still be all too evident: the true, autobiographical, story told in the excellent, multi-award-winning, film *An Angel at my Table* (1990), contains the depiction of an extremely harrowing moment in the New Zealand writer Janet Frame's brief career as a primary school teacher. Her – polite, understated – observer (an inspector, it appears) mostly 'does the right thing' in Janet's classroom yet she is still reduced to a mute, panic-stricken creature who ends up fleeing the classroom (and, sadly, teaching).

The extent to which an observer should participate in a lesson is an interesting question to dwell on. What needs to be negotiated and agreed is whether the mentor will actually participate, and if so, in what ways. Would the trainee wish their observer to 'make up a pair' for example, if pair work has been planned as an activity, and if the attendance in a learner group on the date of the observation results in an uneven number? If supported individual work on tasks is in progress, does the trainee feel that they would value some assistance, so that each learner is more likely to be seen? (Or would they, on the other hand, prefer to get a sense themselves of what having to cope unaided with the challenge of circulating to all twenty students in a group feels like?) If a trainee 'gets stuck', forgets a fact – or gets one badly wrong – should the mentor intervene? If technical problems arise with any of the classroom hardware such as a video monitor should the mentor try to help? More often than not, the answer in these kinds of scenarios will be 'no', and the matter is one to be dealt with at the debriefing stage. However, on occasion a trainee may well happily ask for supportive interventions, and make clear that they would not feel undermined by such. It is simply an issue – one of many in teacher education – on which trying to arrive at a hard and fast ruling is probably unproductive.

Some mentors find it of value to speak to learners (e.g. whilst they are working independently on tasks) to try to ascertain whether they have been enjoying a lesson, and have properly understood the material being taught. This is an especially sensitive area for trainees, however, and definitely ought only to be engaged in if agreement for it has been reached in advance with a trainee. A profound sense of insecurity could result from a trainee not knowing exactly why an observer had started talking to learners in their group.

Some further practical considerations

Much of what follows will perhaps seem simply good sense, while some aspects of the advice could at first sight seem rather difficult to put into practice. However, each of these practical dimensions of observation and debriefing form part of what would now be generally considered essentials.

It is especially important, in particular when conducting a first *formal* observation of a trainee's classroom practice, that mutual agreement has been reached as to which learner group will be involved. This is an especially vulnerable time for many trainees, and it is crucial that they feel they will be seen with a group which will allow them to best demonstrate their developing teaching strengths. Wherever possible, therefore, it is advisable to fall in with the trainee's wishes in this regard.

Clearly, over the course of subsequent observations, it would serve neither the trainee's interests, nor a mentor's, if only those classes – perhaps those posing fewest teaching challenges – were to be observed. In reality, hardly any class should ever be considered 'off limits' as far as observation is concerned. But exceptions do exist, in the form for example of community-based outreach 'single-sex' classes – sometimes provided for women-only groups of language learners, where their participation in learning might be otherwise problematic; teaching such groups is a highly feminised activity in which a male observer's presence would simply run contrary to the spirit of this kind of provision.

In articulating this point of view, mentors might need to draw attention to the fact that being observed with a 'difficult' group need not necessarily be a bad thing, or an event which is inevitably going to drag down the quality of any overall assessment of teaching competence. It does require a particular type of openness to allow an observer into a class where a trainee is experiencing more frustration than 'feelgood'; mentors will need to acknowledge this, praise a trainee's agreement that such a class be seen, and spell out the potential benefits of their having access to an objective view of where and why problems might be arising. (Interestingly, on a number of occasions in the past I have been asked by trainees quite specifically to come in to observe them with classes in which things don't seem to be going at all well; the requests are ones I have always viewed as being only sensible, and evidence of their maturity and resilience.) Some training programmes actually require mentors to construct teaching timetables for trainees which take account not only of levels, target qualifications, etc. but the range of *motivation* seen across different groups. This may well have points in its favour, although mentors often have a sense of protectiveness which steers them away from putting especially hard-to-motivate groups on a trainee's timetable.

As well as agreeing on the teaching group which will be observed, there are such other important considerations involved as the date/notice period which might be appropriate. No trainee, even those with the greatest strengths in their developing skills, reacts well to feeling that an observation has been 'sprung on them'. Wherever possible, a notice period of at least a week is advisable – if trainees say they are happy with less than this then that of course is their decision. (Shorter notice periods may of course, however, not mesh that well with mentors' own schedules and commitments, and it is quite legitimate to point this out.)

A further extremely important factor which needs to be taken into account concerns the importance of observing trainees in a range of *settings* over a course of training. It is not acceptable, or sound practice to, say, only observe someone working in a one-to-one setting (e.g. giving individual support in a college's drop-in centre, or circulating to assist individual learners with independent, project-based, work). On the other hand, only observing a trainee working in lecture mode cannot provide us with any real insights into the confidence they might display in setting up and managing small-group work (or indeed in giving individual support).

Similarly, mentors ought to beware of the risks attached to consistently observing a trainee working only with learners at a very restricted range of qualification levels (or, worst of all, only at *one* level). A PGCE or a CertEd is – at the risk of restating the obvious – a *licence to practise*, and as such can really only legitimately be awarded where competence has been demonstrated in a range of settings. *Equipping our Teachers for the Future* certainly pointed to the need for trainees 'to gain a good understanding of the range of learners in this diverse sector' (DfES, 2004: 11). The ability of trainees to work effectively across such a range (in so far, of course, as it is possible within any one institution) should be being monitored, and supported, by mentors.

Mentors also need to acknowledge that in any one observation there are only so many aspects of classroom competence which can be demonstrated. Textbooks on effective teaching, the nature of the inspection framework and much of the advice provided by trainers all give emphasis to the issue of *variety* (as, overwhelmingly, do learner evaluations of teaching) and accommodating a range of learner preferences within lessons is sometimes seen as the 'holy grail' of good teaching.

In some respects, rather than being positively challenged by all this, trainees can experience a real anxiety that in a particular observed session there will be insufficient evidence for their ability to adopt varied, inclusive, approaches; one hears trainees apologise for there being 'no group work in the lesson today', 'no handout to go with what's being covered' or 'no slides'. What is important is to offer reassurance that it is fully accepted that in, say, a session lasting only 60 or 90 minutes, the range of strategies which can be deployed will not be comprehensive. There will be instances in certain specialisms where the whole of a session may need to be devoted to a single activity. It may be quite legitimate and necessary for a performing arts teacher to sometimes, for example, have her group engaged in intense rehearsal for a forthcoming production. Similarly, in the art and design studio a learner group may need to spend the whole of a session continuing to work on a project brief, and the trainee's role will entirely comprise circulating, monitoring learners' performance, and offering them individual guidance.

It is important, of course, to promote variety (perhaps based on the idea of most learners' attention spans, according to one theorist at least, not being able to cope with an unvaried focus for longer than 20 minutes or so: Buzan, 1982). However, the more important objective to negotiate with trainees should be that of building in variety *over a series* of lessons, so that a group always has the anticipation of different stimuli being on their classroom menu. Attention to the need for such variety can be encouraged by pointing to the way in which a proper, appropriately detailed, scheme of work for a group should include a log of which activities/aids to learning are planned on a week-by-week basis. A separate 'Variety Planner', in grid format, is a very worthwhile alternative, and has the added advantage of giving both trainee and mentor an immediate visual impression of the ways in which one session has differed from another.

The observation itself

The importance of positioning (where to sit) and clarifying the degree of participation (if any) that the observer may have has already been described. Equally important are considerations to do with such things as body language and gesture. Some observers may find it extremely difficult to avoid communicating *non-verbally* that, from their perspective, a lesson is not going as well as they would like. If we aren't able to understand an instruction that a trainee has given to a group, or can't actually see the point of an activity that is being set up, it is all too easy to show our confusion and perplexity. It calls for a surprisingly high degree of self-awareness to know that we are looking puzzled, disappointed or simply generally unhappy with the classroom proceedings we are witnessing. Yet it is really very important that we make strong efforts in this connection, so that the confidence of the person being observed is not undermined. We will probably all at some stage or another, sadly, observe lessons which leave us shaking our head – but must attempt to limit this to a mental process before it becomes a visible, physical, one.

A further challenge lies in balancing the demands of the documentation attached to an observation with actually watching what is going on in the lesson. Occasionally I have heard trainees express real doubts that an observer can possibly have 'properly' seen a lesson in action, because they have spent so much of their time, head down, completing an observation proforma. However, it is true that this kind of criticism has most usually correlated with training schemes that have adopted particularly cumbersome, multi-page, observation documents.

Where the paperwork is indeed complex rather than concise (and the variations seen are many) then there are arguments for simply making handwritten notes which will form the basis of the debriefing, and completing the required forms at a later stage. If this tactic is adopted, however, trainees do need reassuring that the content of any formal report will accurately reflect what was noted and was communicated in the debriefing. Mentors who are fortunate in being able to write speedily and legibly will be able to actually compile formal reports whilst observing (perhaps tidying up/ concluding them while trainees are sending off their groups, gathering up their lesson materials and so on). Some training providers encourage mentors to complete, in-class, electronic versions of observation reports, using tablet PCs, and this facility is particularly worth exploiting in certain circumstances – for example, where a mentor has had to arrange a number of observations on one day.

There is a real skill in being able to juggle between the need to actually see a lesson, especially how learners are responding to it (and from the back of the room it will generally not be at all easy to see their facial expressions, for example) and remaining mindful of what the observation documentation requires of mentors. The situation might be said to be somewhat comparable to taking photographs of events or landscapes, when a concern with correct use of the camera (or, in certain 'tourist' contexts perhaps feeling uncomfortable about using photography at all to 'capture' people and places) is such a preoccupation that the subject itself is at risk of becoming of secondary importance.

Use of timings

It can sometimes be useful to add to observation comments being made occasional in-text or margin notes (much as on a lesson plan) indicating times. In a general sense these can serve to provide additional evidence that mentors were indeed watching classroom proceedings closely. Moreover they can be helpful in allowing a trainee to see, say, where a lesson segment which was ostensibly introductory ran on for an unnecessarily long time, or where a concluding segment including a recapitulation was squeezed into far too little of the lesson as a whole. Any serious misalignments with the proposed timings will also be evident. Also, if a mentor chooses to total up the respective time allocations to teacher talk, student activity, etc. then the proportions of, and balance between, these will similarly stand out.

Use of quotations

Where possible it is sometimes valuable to actually note key phrases from an observed session, whether used by the trainee or a member of a learner group. Mentors can more easily make any necessary debriefing points about e.g. ambiguity of instructions if they have noted down what exactly was said by the trainee – and the kind of reactions manifested by learners ('I'm sorry, can you say all that again please ... did you mean ... ?'). This type of component of an observation report/debriefing is actually of special value in enhancing trainees' learning about their questioning skills, and about the way in which they provide responses to learners' questions. We cannot provide a precise, detailed, account of the classroom interaction in the way that is possible for language-focused research (e.g. a 'Barnes-type' analysis as described in the classic *Language, the Learner and the School*, by Barnes *et al.*, 1969). What we can do, however, is illustrate such interaction at what seem to be key points – of understanding or *mis*understanding – in the session.

Other points to observe

Having been supplied in advance with the *objectives* for a session (and, ideally, having had the chance to discuss these with a trainee) the mentor is able to focus on monitoring progress being made towards meeting these. Were the objectives – perhaps in a paraphrased form – shared with learners? Did the trainee explicitly relate content to these? If segments of what is being taught did not appear to relate well to specified objectives it can be problematic, and learners themselves will quite frequently ask why they were covered in the lesson.

A current 'favourite' of selection panels is to ask an applicant for a teaching post who describes or actually teaches a short lesson the question '... *and how exactly would you know that your objectives had been met?*' This fact, if no other, legitimates a mentor focusing on the *learning checks* which appear to be being used in a session. Are the checks valid, do they cover all the learners in a group? They will not, of course, if only very few group members are targeted in questioning and oral checks such as this are not supplemented by, say, written work. How many learners in a group were questioned? How many were never asked to provide answers? How were flawed responses constructively managed?

There are also broader, rather more impressionistic and difficult to quantify aspects of a trainee's performance which mentors will need to observe. Is the learning 'climate' conducive to participation, or do the members of a group not appear to be comfortable? Does the trainee themselves seem 'at home' in the classroom environment, or at its most extreme is their apparent nervousness actually distracting? Do they have any mannerisms of speech or gesture which may represent distractions? Perhaps most importantly, do they seem to have connected with what is going on in a room – or possess the 'withitness' which a number of observers of teaching feel is crucial in differentiating between effective and ineffective teachers? (This is actually not always that hard to cite evidence for – we have probably all observed at least one class in which the trainee was unaware of a learner reading a magazine or a text message on a mobile phone.)

In connection with these kinds of matters, what mentors can draw attention to, thus adding some objectivity to any comments on what was termed by FENTO during its existence as 'impact and presence', is whether, for instance a trainee has used the classroom space well – have they circulated around the room, signalling to learners that they will be able to note any off-task behaviour? Have they made eye contact well with a group or, on the other hand, 'talked to the board' a lot? How well have they projected their voice? When the lesson was due to start, how exactly did a trainee make their presence felt within a group – what were their strategies for obtaining a quiet start and for signposting the focus and value of the observed session?

The debriefing

It is after the observation, at the debriefing stage, that the contribution mentors can make to the professional learning of trainees is arguably most significant. For this reason it is essential to review a number of key dimensions of the activity, which in some regards calls for especially high levels of skill, self-awareness and sensitivity on the part of mentors. A poorly handled debriefing can even lead to withdrawal from a training programme (this is not an exaggeration, but can be readily documented). On the other hand, a successful one – including one taking place after a quite flawed teaching session – can have profoundly positive effects on a trainee's self-esteem and their developing professional practice.

Some starting points

- ■ Having thanked a trainee for having agreed to the observation, wherever possible the aim should be to try to find at least one thing to say about the lesson, at the very beginning of the debriefing, which sends them a positive message – that it was enjoyable, or at the very least that the material covered was interesting. An acknowledgement that accommodating an observer in a classroom can add to the natural stress of teaching is also worthwhile. And it is always worth taking an early

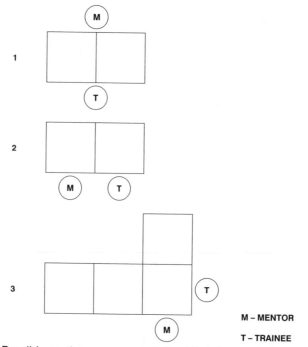

FIGURE 4.2   Possible seating arrangements for debriefings

reading of how the trainee themselves felt the observed lesson had gone ('Well, were you pleased with how that went?')

- If not previously arranged, a time/date should be set as soon as possible for a meeting to discuss the session (unless it is possible to talk immediately after the session, which is of course always the preferred option).
- Privacy is essential, so a venue needs to be available where others will not be able to listen to the conversation.
- So, too, is freedom from interruptions – in so far as this state can ever be achieved in busy institutions. No phone in the room, or one that can be switched off (including, of course, mobile phones), is ideal.
- It is useful to outline what kinds of issues should be covered in the debriefing, including the trainee's own perceptions of a session's strengths and weaknesses.
- The maximum length of the debriefing should be specified.

A seating arrangement should be striven for in which mentor/trainee can make eye contact, while at the same time both look at any relevant notes, diagrams or materials. From Figure 4.2 it will be clear that what usually works best is a situation where the centre point is the corner of a table. (The table can be dispensed with, but it becomes much harder to spread out useful items to which reference is being made.) Sitting opposite each other can promote a 'superior/inferior' relationship, while sitting side by side renders eye contact problematic.

Key components of a successful debriefing

'He was so critical, he never mentioned *anything* which had gone well …': this very real, and sadly often quite frequently repeated – in one variant or another – statement is a useful preface to looking at the substance of the interaction within the debriefing itself. Trainees do seem to be somewhat prone to dwelling on negative points made in the context of debriefing, and it is therefore worth highlighting the value of aiming to find ways in which strengths can be praised. There may have been very few such strengths indeed – in fact, overall, an observed lesson might have been very weak, even one of those where OfSTED might describe any learning which has taken place to have been despite, rather than as a result of, the teacher's presence (OfSTED, 2001).

The challenge here is to make necessary criticisms, even very strong ones, as palatable as they can ever be. We cannot be dishonest and say that a lesson was a success when it clearly was anything but; this would be unprofessional, would jeopardise our own credibility as practitioners and would serve well neither the interests of the trainee nor of their learners. But the kind of – albeit perhaps fairly minimalist – positive statements which can be made to prepare the ground for such strong criticism can include:

- 'It was good to see a punctual start to the session.'
- 'You seem to have spent quite a lot of time preparing your materials for today.'
- 'Your boardwork is very neat and clear.'
- 'I could hear you well at the back of the room.'
- 'Being observed didn't seem to bother you too much.'
- 'It seems you know your material.'
- 'Thanks for letting me have such a helpful plan, and to have been able to place this within the overall scheme of work you also gave me.'

There is, of course, no magical solution should not even any of the above statements apply. In 'worst possible cases' mentors might only have recourse to something along the lines of: 'Well, we've got quite a lot of issues to talk about today, but I hope to be able to make some positive suggestions about each of these.'

In a number of ways, it is possible to summarise the essential 'criticism' elements in debriefings in tabular form. This allows us to note the critical differences between what is usually referred to as *de*structive criticism, as opposed to *con*structive criticism (Table 4.1).

Successful debriefings, as well as simply aiming to incorporate the positive elements shown on the right side of Table 4.1, while avoiding those on the left side, also seem to accord with the following template:

- There is ample space for the trainee's voice to be heard. The useful notion of 'discursive space' allows for a two-way process (the contrast would be with a lecture format event, where e.g. the observer spends the great majority of the debriefing time talking about how they would have taught/would normally teach the session).

TABLE 4.1 Contrasts between constructive and destructive criticism

DESTRUCTIVE CRITICISM	CONSTRUCTIVE CRITICISM
• Tone negative/pessimistic	• Tone optimistic/encouraging
• 'Deficits' drawn attention to (What was not present/covered)	• 'Credits' highlighted (What was accomplished; the strengths of the lesson)
• Largely 'looking back' (as in feedback)	• Looking backwards and forwards (as in 'feed forward')
• What went wrong – all description and no analysis	• Important diagnostic elements – Why might things be going wrong
• Emphasis on observer's own preferred teaching strategies	• Emphasis given to allowing trainee to articulate reasons for their preferences
• Extremely few suggestions made regarding improvements	• A range of 'method' suggestions made, and practical illustrations given of these
• No advice on getting support to make improvements	• Offer of targeted support is prominent in the exchange
• Lesson's every flaw reviewed	• Focus on highlighting why some flaws especially worth correcting
• 'Demolition job' on trainee's self-esteem	• Self-esteem enhancement a priority

- Proceedings include as many questions as possible, ones which encourage trainees to think of alternative strategies and approaches (not single solutions).
- They are based on prioritising issues; not all the flaws in a session will be of equal significance, and the most minor can even actually be overlooked if to include every single failing would produce an overwhelming list of matters for attention.
- Language use is sensitive and culturally aware, but is not so *camouflaged* as to make meaning disappear. Many, if not most of us, aim to be diplomatic, and not blunt, about failings we perceive in others' performance. A self-check on whether this has *only* resulted, however, in a 'camouflage effect' is to simply ask a trainee whether a point is clear, or whether it would be useful to rephrase it.
- The focus is on performance and not personality – the classic advice in this regard is to concentrate on using phrases such as '... and then *what happened was* ...' rather than '... and then *what you did* was ...' Note, though, that this is an especially elusive aspect of conducting effective debriefings. Where it seems virtually impossible to avoid reference to an individual trainee's approach to an element of classroom practice which has seemed ill-judged or poorly handled, it can be perhaps sometimes married to a confession on the mentor's part that they themselves are occasionally still guilty of whatever it is.
- The debriefing's conclusion has two principal parts, a reiteration of any strengths evident in the observed session and agreement regarding the priorities or targets for subsequent observations, signalled by such language as: 'So what, overall,

TABLE 4.2 The learner at the centre

'THE LEARNER PERSPECTIVE'

'THE LEARNER PERSPECTIVE'

One alternative, really quite succinct, framework for providing an overview of an observed lesson is based on a simple set of questions regarding the ways in which a lesson was probably *experienced by learners*:

- What was it likely to have felt like being a student in this lesson?
- Could they see the point of the lesson?
- Did they know what to do, and why they were doing it?
- Were they able to get on with their tasks, in a well-ordered learning environment, or might some learners have been being disrupted by other members of the group?
- Could they see where the lesson fitted into an overall 'scheme of things'?
- Might they have been baffled by any unexplained new terms/ideas?
- Were they clear about if/when their understanding of the lesson's content would be assessed (formally or informally)?
- Would they be likely to value, and actually use, any 'takeaways' – handouts, notes from slides, etc.?
- Were they given any pointers as to how to follow up the lesson independently, e.g. suggested readings, relevant websites?
- Were less confident learners reassured that there would be a chance to revisit the content if it had been found challenging?
- Did they seem to enjoy it?

would you say were the things which we should most concentrate on improving before next time?' or 'Is there anything in particular you feel I could prioritise supporting you with before the next observation?'

It is, furthermore, only good practice for trainees to be invited to follow up any issues on which they have reflected as a result of the debriefing, and/or to get in touch where a specific point does not, after all, seem either clear or valid. This is, after all, only the kind of reassurance we would wish to offer our learner groups after having taught them a topic or skill.

One clear advantage which this approach carries with it is that it obviously accords well with the emphasis being placed by the inspectorate and colleges themselves on 'placing the learner at the heart' of what is being done in post-compulsory education. However, it is presented here merely as a basis for thinking about how to debrief a trainee, and cannot encompass all the *details* that will need to come into the mentor–trainee interaction following an observation.

Debriefing is perhaps one of those dimensions of the mentoring role where the *artistry* of teaching itself comes into play. We can conceive of a 'formula' or a 'template' such as those as are described above, which will allow us to structure the event. But from certain perspectives the risk we run is of a mechanistic approach, where the ability of experienced, competent, practitioners to operate on the basis of an informed intuition – their autonomous professional judgement, one might say – is discounted, or at any rate marginalised. Effective debriefing can only be formulaic, i.e. based on 'science', up to a point. It entails knowledge not only of teaching a subject but of oneself, a real facility with sensitive oral communication and an ability to listen to and to empathise with an individual who may be experiencing some stress. In these ways mentors who have had any exposure at all to certain principles used in counselling are probably advantaged in undertaking their responsibilities, but in so far as 'crafting' a successful debriefing is concerned the motivation to do so is finally what may be most important. It is in this *creative* sense that I have therefore invoked above the idea of 'artistry', as I did in Chapter 3 in the context of professional learning.

Some cautions

If we accept just how crucially important observation and debriefing are in the mentoring relationship, certain cautions may be worth providing.

The use of email in providing feedback

It would be extremely blinkered to fail to recognise the ways in which electronic communications have, in certain ways, been conducive to convenience and the saving of time and expense. In its important statement on 'equipping our teachers for the future' the Department for Education and Skills points to 'e-mentoring' as having a role to play in the mix of functions performed by mentors (DfES, 2004: 15).

Yet many people do experience disquiet over some of the more negative consequences of the use of this medium. The neglect of basic courtesies, and the use sometimes of really quite abrasive language (which would have been less likely to be encountered, it is claimed, in 'snail mail' or conversations – at any rate between professionals) have been drawn attention to. Using email to provide feedback on an observed lesson may, therefore, carry certain risks. Mentors should beware of a harsher tone creeping in, with points being made hurriedly and with less care to construct the sort of tactful, 'kinder' phrasing which face-to-face communication might entail.

Neglect of the liaison function

Although in this section the need for privacy has been noted (in the context of a venue for debriefings) this should not imply that information relating to classroom practice cannot be appropriately shared. Liaison with training institutions is essential, in fact. Where a college-based mentor is able to identify targets for a trainee, monitoring of progress in working towards these will be most efficient where any other individual involved in the trainee's programme (usually a HE-based tutor) is apprised of these. (The process should obviously also work in the opposite direction.) Mentors have a responsibility to share the outcomes of observations with certain other key figures – always taking pains to first communicate to the trainee that this will be taking place, and the reasons for the liaison being a valuable part of the training programme.

Overlong lists of 'areas for improvement'

These can be counterproductive: Where a trainee's practice has caused concern in a number of regards there must subsequently take place an intelligent selection and ordering of points needing attention. One criterion useful in the construction of such a 'shortlist' is simply how urgent something is. Ought it to be remedied before the very next meeting with a learner group? Some examples might be extreme inaudibility, illegible boardwork, late arrival of a trainee with no apology provided to a group ... these are all aspects of practice which might have fairly immediate negative consequences, including causing learners to withdraw from their course. Are there some less serious concerns which can either be listed separately, or 'saved up'? A listing of, say, a dozen problems can seem an insurmountable obstacle to a trainee, who may be demotivated enough by the experience of being given such a list to even abandon the idea of teaching.

Unrealistic expectations

These may unconsciously interpenetrate mentors' feedback. Avoiding this syndrome calls for a high level of self-awareness, in particular being able to recall being challenged by classroom situations oneself whilst still a practitioner with only limited experience. The terminology used by a number of training providers, that of *'beginning teacher'* is actually quite helpful as it signifies that a trainee's professional journey is only just beginning. Mistakes which might appear plain stupid to a teacher with ten years' classroom experience are quite often eminently forgivable ones in someone who has only perhaps taught for a total of six hours. In this context, referring to the parallel of craft *apprenticeships* might be helpful, especially as it is arguably true that a trainee is in reality the 'apprentice' to the mentor – the 'master' of their craft, to pursue the analogy using the most traditional (but in some senses possibly becoming rather archaic) terminology.

Initial teacher education in the UK is incredibly short when compared to the kind of preparation for a craft which, at least in the past, entailed up to five years of apprenticeship – the length of time which my own father, for one, spent in becoming a skilled carpenter and joiner. Trainees on pre-service courses are in training typically for a mere eight months (and on some universities' programmes will not teach at all for the first three months of this, i.e. the autumn term). Even towards the end of this kind of period it is neither realistic nor legitimate to expect the kind of confidence and 'polish' which a 'time-served' craftsman might have been expected to display. We can, in other words, expect to see a developing *competency*, but it is highly unlikely that we will witness *mastery*.

To some extent, another perspective which seems to offer mentors a valuable starting point when contemplating how to approach observations and debriefings is that of 'value added'. The arguments in favour of including such a measure in arriving at judgements of school and college learners, alongside their raw scores in tests and exams, will be well known by experienced practitioners. While we cannot adopt the kinds of statistical methods used to demonstrate that learners' achievements – their 'distance travelled' – were frequently more impressive than their results would lead commentators to believe, we can certainly think in terms of trainees' *baselines*. Individual trainees will all start from different points – e.g. in terms of level of confidence, their intuitive grasp of what learners will best respond to, the depth and breadth of their subject knowledge and so on. If we acknowledge the importance of such baselines it allows for a reorientation of feedback towards an emphasis on *progress made*.

The issue of grading

Part of the process of *socialising* trainees into the nature of PCET realities is introducing them to the nature of the grading system currently used in the assessment and inspection of practical teaching. In general both pre- and in-service training programmes now require that in connection with at least some of the observations conducted by tutors and/or mentors a grade be awarded. For some mentors, this will be a possibly contentious, perhaps onerous, aspect of their role – and the legitimacy of applying a national body's criteria to *beginning* teachers in particular may indeed be questionable. Nevertheless, if grading is to be undertaken it is advisable to stress that

a. in most respects mentors' evaluative comments, not a grade, will best inform the trainee's reflections and strategies for improvement;
b. a grade does not equate in any way to a static, immutable, state of affairs but only to performance on one day, with a particular learner group; and
c. from an analysis of grades awarded over time it emerges that very few 'top' grades indeed (grade '1's) have been recorded.

Mentors should be aware, however, that trainees being awarded 'lesser' grades such as 'only' '3' ('satisfactory', in most formulations) – which from most perspectives would be a perfectly respectable outcome in the context of traineeship – can sometimes feel aggrieved; it seems almost as if this particular grade is subconsciously being compared to honours degree class, i.e. 'a third'.

Hostile reactions to feedback

Most mentors will from time to time have to contend with trainees whose reaction to feedback, however skilfully this is given, is quite hostile, possibly even confrontational. There is a range of possible explanations for this state of affairs. One might simply be that a mentor is considerably younger than the person they are mentoring: many new entrants to PCET teaching, especially those from vocational backgrounds, are fairly mature – perhaps in their forties or even fifties. (At the time of writing there is interest in some quarters in the possibility of recruiting higher numbers of individuals who have served in the armed forces – a group who might conceivably need a particularly aware approach.) Receiving criticism from a relatively youthful mentor can in itself be hard to adjust to. It is also sometimes said that gender can perhaps be a factor in negative situations which develop between mentor and trainee; most usually the situation being described involves a mature male being mentored by a younger female.

To a large extent, though, we are in the realms of conjecture here. What is probably easier to recognise is the simple fact that when we are commenting on someone's teaching they can experience this as reflecting on their identity as human beings. This is why the need to emphasise aspects of practice, avoiding wherever possible seeming to personalise criticism, is so important. So, too, is adequately setting the scene for observation/debriefing, and making quite clear to trainees that the process is intended to be, above all else, a supportive one, aimed at improving the experience of both trainees and their learners.

It is worth illustrating for trainees the kinds of 'Yes, but ...' responses which might be given to feedback, which are so unproductive. A trainee saying what 'normally'/'would have'/'could have' featured, in a lesson, had events of some kind or another not conspired against them is, more often than not, a form of self-defence – what mentors need to ensure, therefore, is that they stress that they are not in the business of 'attack'.

I am not here advocating aiming for a quiet life by manipulating trainees in such a way that they never interrogate a mentor's criticism, but will simply agree with everything being said to them. This would not be developmental in any way, as the trainee's responses will be purely 'strategic' ones – i.e. they will be being made to 'get the mentor off their back', and to appear cooperative. What we must seek are 'learning' responses, ones which are based on a genuine acceptance of points and guidance being provided by mentors.

All of the above hinges, to reiterate this centrally important point, on the effective provision by the mentor of a rationale for observation and debriefing, and then sharing appropriate guidance (ground rules, some might say) regarding ways in which feedback should be most positively both given and responded to. Stressful exchanges might still arise, and perhaps even cause a mentor to seek support from his or her peers in dealing with these. But there are certainly some steps at least which individual mentors can take to mitigate the likelihood of conflict with a trainee arising.

Failing to see trainees as individuals

> Like every other teacher, you and I are individuals with personalities of our own and teaching approaches which are special to us. Certainly no one can take over another teacher's ways lock, stock and barrel, apply them, and hope for success.
>
> (Marland, 1975: 3)

Although Michael Marland's long-standard work on survival in classrooms for new teachers does go on to remind readers of the existence of a body of transferable principles and techniques, he is right, in underscoring the individuality which teaching, perhaps above all professions, allows for. He is, to use phrasing with a greater degree of modernity, warning of the dangers of attempting to clone new teachers in our own likeness.

When describing the kind of mentoring they hope to receive, many trainees express sentiments closely according with these:

What I hope for from my mentor: support, encouragement, genuine concern for my development. I hope that my mentor will be able to strike the right balance between guiding my learning and allowing me to develop my own ideas and my own teaching style.

(Trainee, full-time pre-service course, 2004)

Here we can see that already at the very earliest stages – the quotation was obtained during the first weeks of a trainee's programme – there is a duality of needing pointers, but not prescription. The word 'balance' seems of special importance, as used by this trainee. They appear fully accepting of a mentor's role in imparting the benefits of their own experience, and acknowledge the credibility of the mentor to offer guidance. But they are also already finding their own voice, and in an important sense asking that this be heard.

The message for mentors in this far from untypical statement need not be laboured – it is simply that (perhaps especially in the context of giving feedback) we should be self-aware enough to judge whether our views are being overly influenced by our own pedagogic preferences. Are we really looking at 'mistakes' – of style or substance – or is it sometimes merely a case of 'Well, it's not really me'? Are approaches which are different from our own always inferior? If something is working, but perhaps surprisingly so, does it threaten us in some way because of this fact?

As observed elsewhere in this guide, mentors should neither be aiming at standardising professional practice, nor presenting single-strategy solutions to problems in learning and teaching. An absolutely fundamental dimension of effective mentoring relationships exists in the plane of generating discursive knowledge about *alternatives*. Clearly we have the responsibility to exercise our professional judgement – and authority – where it is evident that actual harm may be being done to learners by a trainee's approach. But if advice being given is based solely on the desire to reproduce ourselves as teachers (and possibly also to reproduce our own 'best' teachers, often those who inspired us, earlier on, to enter the profession) then we will struggle to justify this position.

The list of cautions provided here is certainly not intended to be comprehensive. As with virtually all of the components of mentoring, a high degree of learning on the job will come into play with regard to what works well/less well in the observation and discussion of trainees' classroom practice. So, too, will the collaboration and sharing of experience with other mentors that is being strongly advocated at various points in this guide.

References

The first book on this list, from 1969, as well as Michael Marland's from 1975, will appear decidedly 'vintage' to some readers. However, they are considered by many to be classics and I for one believe that much of what they have to say remains of very high value. Nicholas Otty's 1972 review of his own teacher training year is not only very enjoyable, it is also insightful. I therefore make no apologies for the inclusion of any of these here.

Barnes, D., Britton, J., and Rosen, R. (1969) *Language, the Learner and the School*, Harmondsworth: Penguin.

Buzan, T. (1982) *Use Your Head*, London: Ariel.

Cunningham, B. (2000) Beginning 'close encounters': on starting to teach in colleges, *Teacher Development*, 4/3: 241–56.

DfES (2004) *Equipping our Teachers for the Future: Reforming Initial Teacher Training for the Learning and Skills Sector*, Nottingham: Department for Education and Skills.

Marland, M. (1975) *The Craft of the Classroom*, London: Heinemann Educational Books.

OfSTED (2003) *The Initial Training of Further Education Teachers: A Survey*, London: Office for Standards in Education.

OfSTED/ALI (2001) *The Common Inspection Framework*, London: Office for Standards in Education/Adult Learning Inspectorate.

Otty, N. (1972) *Learner Teacher*, Harmondsworth: Penguin.

University of East London (2010) *Cass School of Education Programme Handbook, PGCE (PCET) 2010-2011*, London: University of East London.

Wragg, E. C. (1999) *An Introduction to Classroom Observation* (2nd edn), London: Routledge

The rewards and challenges of mentoring

Chapter objectives

- to indicate the range of professional rewards and challenges which mentors will encounter.

> Overall my mentor has been a great support. I will always appreciate his advice, and will take all I have learnt to my new jobs.
>
> (Trainee teacher qualifying from a full-time, pre-service, course in July 2004)

The rewards

I would like to begin this chapter by paraphrasing a once very well known advertising slogan used to attract new entrants to school teaching, and say that quite simply *everyone remembers a good mentor*. Clearly the view of the trainee quoted above underscores this claim, and it is a highly affirming way of perceiving the value of this part of an experienced teacher's professional work.

Mentoring is an activity which has almost unparalleled potential to shape the developing skills – and attitudes – of teachers in training. The support given to someone in the early stages of their teaching career will be remembered and valued, very probably for the rest of their professional life. This fact is in itself satisfying – and so often, in my experience, it is evidenced by the ways in which new teachers frequently stay in touch with the individuals who have mentored them, providing occasional updates on career progression and personal matters.

Clearly, however, mentors would want to have some further positive reasons for committing themselves to the role, given that it is a time-consuming additional duty. It has perhaps been squeezed in alongside a teaching timetable comprising, say, twenty-five hours' weekly classroom contact and all the usual range of functions now normally expected of established PCET teachers.

One dimension of the activity which we can, with some confidence, draw attention to is that, in the main, the new entrants to teaching are able, committed and well qualified; they are, therefore, individuals with whom a positive professional relationship is a strong likelihood. They are people it is in our interests to properly induct and socialise because they have a great deal to offer to the profession and to their learners. Helping them adjust to the realities of post-compulsory education, so that trainees may begin as soon as is possible to begin to make valuable contributions, is in itself fulfilling.

Some trainees may have held preconceptions about the nature of the sector (although this is very unlikely if they themselves are former PCET students, e.g. having studied on Access courses) and these kinds of issues can act as barriers to their integration into the community of practice that they aspire to join. Of course, some of the 'realities' might be quite hard to present in positive vein, and sometimes it can be difficult to safeguard against contaminating early impressions of the sector with negativity – I am thinking here about such issues as the long-standing lack of parity with school teachers in terms of salary, for instance, or the intrusive form which management strictures regarding student retention and achievement can assume. The sheer volume of paperwork which burdens not just college teachers but those working in every phase of education is probably quite hard for mentors to be positive about.

However, it is perhaps useful to note that in McKelvey and Andrews' study of the perceptions and motivations of trainees, many of the individuals surveyed viewed the acknowledged challenges faced by college teachers as positive ones, and had actually been attracted to the idea of making their mark in a challenging profession. This particular study, furthermore, found that where trainees 'had been well supported by their personal mentors [this] had strengthened their commitment to teaching in FE' (McKelvey and Andrews, 1998: 362).

For new entrants with a more limited degree of awareness of what the concerns, norms and preoccupations of the sector are, there will probably be a sense of disorientation during their first period of contact with real PCET students, and on witnessing the sometimes frenetic – and occasionally beleaguered – lives lived by full-time teachers. Assisting in shortening any time during which such trainees experience disorientation is a hugely important, and surely satisfying, function for mentors to perform. The kind of 'jargon busting' advocated in Chapter 2 can play an important part in this, along with attending to all the small 'housekeeping' matters that someone entering any new occupation or institution will need to become familiar with – where these are dealt with early on then the phrase 'at home' will more often than not be just the right one to describe how a trainee will rapidly come to feel.

I believe we can also draw attention to such positive reasons for committing to mentoring as those which follow, some of which are further developed in the concluding section of this guide, pointing to the links between mentoring and continuing professional development.

Recognition by an institution of one's own professionalism

This professionalism includes both classroom skills and the ability to maintain effective relations with colleagues. There is a certain status attached to mentoring, and a clear source of professional pride. At a particular college mentors are described (in the college's mentoring policy) as being

- regarded by his or her peers with credibility and respect [and]
- regarded by his or her line manager as a good role model

(West Kent College,[1] n.d.).

Understanding one's own practice

There are benefits deriving from being stimulated to make plain to a trainee the *why* as well as the *what* of a particular approach to teaching. All mentors are involved in representing and explaining their own practice, and in doing so are caused to move well beyond 'I've always done it this way'. They are steered into analysing the 'it', and interrogating their usual strategies for getting learners to discern something interesting, and conceptually manageable, in 'it'. Mentors, to put it slightly differently, stand to *learn* more about why certain approaches work well, where others might not, in the very act of having to '*teach*' the underlying principles to their trainees. The task here for the mentor is centred on making accessible to a trainee the essentials of the *tacit* knowledge they hold.

Satisfaction in helping new entrants to survive

There are satisfactions to be gained from assisting in practical, and less practical, ways new entrants to teaching to survive what is undoubtedly a demanding environment. Huberman, in writing about how teachers 'survive' their early experiences describes how 'on the other side of the ledger, the *discovery* theme [includes] having one's own pupils, one's own classroom, materials … and of feeling oneself a colleague among peers' (Huberman, 1992: 122). It is by facilitating what Huberman refers to as discovery that mentors can bring about for trainees a situation, a state of emotional well-being almost, that allows them to tolerate what he depicts as 'survival'. At the core of Huberman's formulation of what it means to discover the positives of professional life as a teacher is probably quite simply 'feeling at home': included in the life of an institution – a positive outcome which no one is better placed to bring about than mentors, it might be claimed.

Extension of one's own repertoire

Experienced mentors often happily acknowledge the ways in which their own repertoire of teaching skills and ideas has been extended by contact with a trainee. (Similarly university tutors will readily talk about the good new ideas being tried out in the classrooms where they are observing their trainees, and which they themselves will experiment with in future.)

Jackson has described some of the key components of teacher development as relating to 'looking at teaching differently, seeing it in a new light, coming to appreciate its complexity more than we have done as yet' (Jackson, 1992: 67). This kind of process appears to me to be an entirely positive one, which might well be triggered by working with a trainee. So, too, would be the – at first sight somewhat sad – outcome of 'possibl[y] develop[ing] a more hesitant manner, a kind of *pedagogical stammer*, as a result of our reflection and newly won insight' (ibid.; emphasis added).

This kind of especially interesting argument was also advanced by Healy and Welchert (1990), who held that mentoring is fundamentally a *reciprocal* relationship, in which there are potential benefits for both mentor and trainee; it has the potential to be a 'transformative' experience for both. It is distinguishable 'from other superior/ subordinate interactions', in having for the trainee the object of 'the achievement of an identity transformation, a movement from the status of understudy to that of self-directing colleague', while for the mentor the relationship may be 'a vehicle for achieving midlife "generativity", meaning a *transcendance of stagnating self-preoccupation*' (ibid., p. 17; emphasis added).

Put simply, trainees derive professional learning from what mentors are passing on to them, but this interaction itself may lead to a growth in mentors' own understanding of their professionalism and their motivation – and self-esteem, in all probability. This last point was succinctly put by one of the respondents in a fairly recent study of mentors and their selection for the role: 'it helped to make me feel more valued' (Cunningham, 2004: 276).

ICT skills

As well as novel approaches to classroom practice, many recently qualified trainees will now be bringing with them a facility with ICT-derived learning materials, and even innovative pedagogies associated with ICT, from which many mentors may learn much of value. Can 'old dogs' learn new tricks? It will depend on their receptivity to these.

Professional development opportunities

The kinds of professional development opportunities which may stem from gaining experience as a mentor are not insignificant. These may include opportunities to contribute more extensively to staff training and development activities, or to assume a fuller range of supervisory functions in college. Some colleges do appear to be successful in promoting mentoring, describing it in terms of being a valuable career development for staff hoping for career progression into roles where they can demonstrate their experience of working with staff in a supportive role. Many mentors have found their experience to be seen as highly relevant by universities seeking to recruit new teacher trainers. (These kinds of themes, especially, are further developed in Chapter 8.)

Fundamentally, what the activity of mentoring has as its end product is the enhancement of the experiences of a highly diverse range of learners. The person who has been supportively mentored will work more effectively, and with greater insight, as a result of the guidance they have received, and the ultimate beneficiaries of this will be their learners. The vision outlined in *Equipping our Teachers for the Future* talks about the 'direct impact' which teacher training has right across the range of post-compulsory provision, including for example:

- the key skills that underpin success in education, lifelong learning and personal development;
- the attainment levels of young people and their aspirations to enter higher education, and courses such as Foundation Degrees

(DfES, 2004a: 5).

Mentors can, rightly I believe, accord themselves much credit in these kinds of contexts.

Certain of the above rewards can of course serve to emphasise the ways in which mentor–trainee relations are potentially not exclusively 'one-way', or 'giving–taking' interactions. There can often be a rewarding mutuality in the exchange. In a number of respects it seems there is real potential for the professional learning which takes place within the setting of the mentoring relationship to apply to both parties. The interesting Guile and Lucas notion of a 'learning professional' (Guile and Lucas, 1999) would appear to accommodate this process, as one of the dimensions of professional life which takes us beyond reflective practice – at least in the relatively minimalist, predominantly introspective and retrospective, mode that they critiqued. The professional identity of 'learning professionals' appears to owe much to their *receptivity to ideas*. Such professionals show obvious capacities for listening to, and learning from, the communities they serve – in our present context the communities are both those of new entrants to teaching, and of the learners within PCET.

There is also, it seems, scope for avoiding as an established professional the kind of disengagement or bitterness which Michael Huberman has reviewed in his work on teachers' life-spans (or 'life cycles'). With a commendable tentativeness, Huberman wonders whether mature teachers sometimes display a tendency to 'withdraw' – perhaps, citing Becker, because of frustrated ambitions or 'plateauing' in the profession. This kind of process may be about disengaging 'from policies and practices of which one disapproves … [or] a response to pressures from the environment to cede one's place to younger colleagues and fresher ideas' (Huberman, 1992: 126).

Engaging in mentoring, one might argue, could militate against these negatives, and entail a degree of professional renewal – or at least achievement of the 'serenity' (ibid., p. 127) that Huberman viewed as an alternative to bitterness. For some readers, this kind of formulation may seem to somewhat overdramatise what lies in store – negative or positive – for long-term teachers, but I would argue that the perspective is not all that difficult to connect with a discussion of reasons why mentoring might hold benefits for mentors as well as trainees.

The challenges

It would be a 'straightforward' approach to summing up mentoring's challenges if one simply tried to categorise these as being either practical, professional or personal – such a beguiling, alliterative, schema might indeed have its proponents. However, in reality there are quite often very fuzzy lines between the ways in which mentors can experience a sense of being challenged. For example, the 'professional' challenge of managing a difficult post-observation debriefing can easily shade into the intensely personal one of having to attempt to 'switch off' after what can sometimes be an extremely stressful event to allow for some kind of relatively untroubled home life. And, somewhere in most mentors' thinking, questions of *ethics* will at some stage arise – an example of this might be where teaching of such a worryingly ineffective (possibly even damaging) nature has been observed in a trainee that a mentor finds themselves pondering whether to become a 'whistleblower' and rapidly alert a training institution to what they have witnessed. Such questions can derive from any of the realms we might be tempted to separate out as being either practical, professional or personal in nature.

Probably the easiest challenge to identify in the life of a mentor is simply finding *time* to engage in the activity. In an ideal world, mentors would probably all have been given a reduction in the amount of time they are required to be available for other duties. (See Chapter 1's proposal to this effect.) In general, colleges do not expect teachers to assume personal tutor responsibilities without formally structuring this activity into their timetable, and in certain regards a case could be made for the same sort of principle to apply to mentoring – as it does in some institutions at least.

Where the time demands of mentoring are not, however, formally acknowledged in this way it will call for a particularly skilled approach to time management, and real awareness of trainees' anxieties over not having enough time to discuss their concerns, and their developing practice, with mentors. Mentors may have to 'state the obvious' and spell out that they typically spend their days 'multi-tasking', with teaching, meetings, paperwork and – often – middle-management responsibilities competing with mentoring for their attention. Trainees will not, certainly early on in the relationship, always connect automatically with just how busy a mentor may be; they may well need e.g. an explanation as to why a post-observation debriefing might have to take place at the end of a day rather than immediately after the end of a lesson (a situation such as will arise where a mentor then has two lessons of their own to teach, for instance!).

A highly relevant aspect of the boundary setting advocated in this guide will be the necessity to frame, in advance of key meetings, the period which it will be possible to allocate to them: 'We'll have roughly half an hour, if we start promptly at 4 o'clock, just after my own class ends.'

Role conflict

Mentors may be challenged by issues arising as a result of *role conflict*. This may well be especially likely where a trainee is failing to make satisfactory progress against targets which have been set for them. The principal reason role conflict may arise has much to do with a potential tension between mentors wishing to accentuate the nurturing, supportive, dimensions of the role, whilst at the same time needing to acknowledge their role in assuring high standards of learning and teaching. Mentors adhering to a strongly humanistic, Rogerian, educational philosophy may be especially challenged. They are *assessing performance*, and so long as this function has to be carried out (see below) it will set certain limits on the extent to which they can allow the type and pace of a trainee's professional learning to be wholly self-determined.

In cases where mentors are beginning to have concerns about a trainee's progress they may be torn between wanting to 'give the benefit of the doubt' – to wait a while longer to see where improvements based on advice begin to be evident – and, on the other hand, will be aware that training institutions typically insist on the earliest possible reporting of such concerns. Should they 'send in the "cause for concern" form' or not? This kind of scenario will be but one of the many which will challenge the professional judgement, and the overall professionalism, of mentors.

Official, i.e. institutional, endorsement of mentoring as an activity is most usually, I would contend, born out of a mixture of altruism and pragmatism on the part of managers. The former stimulates a search for individuals whose approachability and good interpersonal skills can be seen as likely to give *trainees* the best experience they can hope for; the latter seeks experienced staff who will, first and foremost, see the quality of *student* learning, and achievement levels, as standing to gain most from the supportive work they will undertake with trainees.

As so often the dichotomy here may, however, be a false one – a contented trainee who feels that their potential is being nurtured, and that their professional standards are developing, is not in some way a polar opposite of a group of learners who are achieving their educational aims. There is a convincing case for arguing that the two things are strongly interrelated. And mentors who are able to operate as *critical friends* are those most likely to strengthen and deepen the relationship between trainee development and learner achievement. In practical terms, being a critical friend entails balancing the kind of psychosocial support for a trainee (which probably leads them to describe a mentor's friendship and approachability) with being able to offer such criticism as is needed to ensure that learners' achievements do not suffer as a result of exposure to habitually ineffective practice. Offering criticism *constructively* will not cause trainees to lose any professional respect – or liking – they may have shown towards a mentor.

It is understandable that mentors can experience certain tensions in the role – they can never, after all, be solely concerned with any one single focus, whether this be offering curriculum advice, organising a programme of classes for a trainee to teach or whatever. These activities will always be found associated with evaluative functions, and those related to the assessment of practice. Cox, writing on 'teacher as mentor', draws attention to the 'tension *generated by the assessment function* of the mentor' (Cox, 1996: 42, cited in Huddleston and Unwin, 2007: 185; my emphasis). Cox was, in fact, arguing for a wider adoption of peer or collaborative mentoring to address what she saw as a problematic 'imbalance of power' (ibid.) and such arrangements as she suggests do have a number of positive benefits. However, within the specific context of the current training framework it is a fact that both mentors and trainees will need to continue to live with a degree of 'tension', and manage this as professionally as possible.

Ultimately, mentors under present statutory arrangements covering training for, and entry to, the profession of PCET teacher are also in a gatekeeping role, to some extent. Some may find this a worrying realisation, but others may, on the other hand, find it one which further enhances their professional self-esteem: playing a part in raising the level of teaching quality is a significant, and laudable, contribution.

Boundary setting

Mentors may be challenged by the need to try to set certain boundaries around the interaction they must have with their trainees. Some such boundaries will not need to be agonised over as they will be to a large extent specified by the structure and regulations of whatever training programme is being followed – 'How many hours per week must I ensure this person teaches?' 'How many times per term must I observe them?' 'What procedure must I follow if their attendance/punctuality record drops below X%?' All of these kinds of questions are likely to be susceptible to clear, easy to locate, answers. Other questions will, at first sight, have answers which are slightly fuzzier, and some of these will in fact need to be negotiated with trainees. The issue of *mentor availability* has already been referred to, but is worth underlining as it causes so many grievances where trainees do not perceive that it has been made explicit by individual mentors just what is going to be feasible in terms of frequency/length/times of meetings. This area should be clarified at the earliest stage, taking pains to ensure that trainees understand and sympathise with the reasons why an offer may appear to be less generous than they might have been anticipating.

Communicating with trainees

Certain of the above boundaries are specifically to do with *communication*, and are of major significance. The modes in which mentor and trainee communicate with each other, and the purposes for which they communicate, will all need sensible discussion early on. For example, if mentors feel it will be efficient to allow trainees to have their personal phone numbers (so that they might, say, discuss any emergency cover arrangements necessitated by a trainee's illness) up to what time at night will it be acceptable to make contact? How 'routine' ought it to be that a trainee contacts a mentor at the weekend to talk through their ideas for lessons they are to teach first thing on Monday morning? If a trainee is to be invited to use email to raise queries with their mentor, what kind of typical response time might they be advised of? (An assumption that is so often made is that almost instantaneous replies will be sent – as if we are all permanently watching our inbox.)

These are questions about which it is not that constructive for trainers, managers, or other parties to attempt to legislate on. They require case-by-case discussion between mentor/trainee, and the agreement of fair, manageable boundaries; if these are not arrived at, a good deal of ill-will on both sides can be generated.

Internal and external locus of control

The apparent difficulty some trainees have in accepting criticism (especially, but not only, when seeing it as 'destructive') was largely dealt with in connection with observations. However, a further idea which it is worth touching on here can be related to such difficulties when they seem to arise for a trainee over *any* issues which are raised with them. Such issues might, for example, be to do with such matters as poor attendance at team meetings ('No one ever informs me about these') or routinely causing student complaints by returning their marked work late ('But most of them give it in late anyway'). Mentors, should we need to remind ourselves, are responsible for supporting trainees in every aspect of their developing professionalism, not just their classroom competence. They are thus exposed to the stresses and strains of possibly having to make criticisms of any one of a number of dimensions of a trainee's performance within an institution. For this reason it may in some respects be helpful to have recourse to a possible explanation of quite why it is that some trainees 'handle' such criticisms so poorly.

The trainee who appears incapable of ever accepting that the responsibility for some aspect of their underperformance must rest primarily with them is often an extremely challenging individual with whom to work. This is the trainee who will always seek to find reasons 'beyond their control' for why things are going wrong. Probably every reader of this guide will be able to recognise the person who will never readily admit responsibility for (in)actions on their part, and for whom other individuals (or systems, structures or events) are almost invariably to blame. On the other hand, mentors may work with trainees who are usually far less challenging because they will acknowledge their own part in events – they do not claim a passive victimhood, and can normally accept at least a part of the blame for whatever it has been found necessary to criticise.

The contrasts between such trainees may sometimes be explicable in terms of their having either an internal *locus of control* or one which is external. As will probably already have been surmised from the terminology used here, it is the trainee whose response to criticism (and to events in general) is essentially to 'point the finger of blame' elsewhere who is operating with an *external* locus of control. The course of events is perceived as being determined wholly by factors external to themselves. Therefore they are liable to ask, for instance, 'What could I do about *that*?' – and are also likely to dismiss most answers to their 'question' as being unworkable in one way or another. Far less stressful for mentors are the trainees who seem able to discern *in themselves* an appropriate degree of responsibility for something which has (or hasn't) taken place. The *internal* locus of control possessed by such individuals allows them to see that they are *not* powerless to influence the course of events, and that it is unfair and inappropriate to routinely depict other individuals or agencies as being to blame for things that have gone wrong. These, then, are the trainees who, hearteningly, will *most readily take a high degree of responsibility for effecting improvements in their professional behaviours.*

Possible tensions over 'flexibility'

Although it may appear a rather flippant observation to make, in some regards 'flexibility' seems to have become the PCET sector's 'F-word'. Institutions have had to be flexible – or 'nimble' – in finding new learners, new sources of funding, creatively seeking out potential links with employers and so on. And teachers have had to become increasingly flexible over matters such as the length and structure of their working week, the location of some of their work (e.g. when they are required to deliver customised workplace training in-house, i.e. at an employer's chosen site) and, perhaps most significantly in relation to the theme of the present section of this guide, in connection with the very subjects they teach. All those who are familiar with the changes witnessed in PCET in the past two decades or more will be able to think of such examples as the geography teacher who has had to 'reinvent' him or herself as a teacher of travel and tourism, the specialist in maths and physics now working predominantly in numeracy, or the literature graduate spending much time each week assisting learners with their study skills.

A proportion of new entrants to PCET teaching will be aware of the ways in which they will need to be flexible over what they teach, where and when they are to teach it, and with what size of learner group (see below): they are, as I have already alluded to, sometimes former PCET students themselves, so will have gained a sense of the realities of the sector. Others, however, will find the demands of teaching evening classes, or working in curriculum areas not necessarily even all that clearly related to their initial specialisms, unsettling to varying degrees. (A third category of individuals, such as one recent sociology graduate I met, are actually positive about extending their range – in this particular case by taking on a timetable including very significant amounts of business studies teaching: they respond constructively to the challenge of rapidly acquiring a new body of content knowledge, and to the notion of 'adding a new string to their bows', especially with an eye to their future employment.)

With the above syndrome in mind, what mentors have increasingly had to engage with is the task of organising for a trainee a timetable that will sometimes inevitably take them some distance away from a shared – 'loved', even – specialism. There may be an element in this of tensions between loyalty to one's subject, and responsibility towards a trainee – for whom it would be a disservice to shield them from what has become a notable feature of the PCET landscape. Where mentors have themselves had to cross subject boundaries, and/or work at 'lower' levels than they had previously, then possibly the kind of tension I am describing here will not be especially problematic.

Rather similarly, PCET teachers have had to become, it seems, ever more flexible with regard to the size of learner groups with which they are asked to work; the appealingly small size of groups I myself taught in the 1980s – often comprising only around 10–12 students – is now rare. Many mentor/practitioners will lament this fact, and may find it relatively hard to extol for their trainees the merits of working with groups of, say, 20+ learners. The pressures that have led us to the present state of affairs are several, and have been much described over the years – rising enrolments, reduced numbers of FE colleges and managements being concerned to amalgamate into larger groups any that on financial grounds are deemed to be too small to be viable are all elements that come into the frame.[2]

'Letting go'

For what are often the most positive, supportive motives imaginable, mentors may sometimes simply take far too much upon their own shoulders when they work with trainees (as they may have already displayed a tendency to do in their work with college learners/their personal tutees, perhaps). Most trainees require a lot of 'hand-holding' in the early stages of a mentoring relationship, and weaker trainees will take longer than others to wean off a highly intensive process which makes great demands on mentors' time and energies. However, what is important is to articulate at a point in the relationship judged by the mentor to be most appropriate that the frequency/ intensity of contact will be diminishing, that the degree of monitoring (e.g. of lesson plans, learning materials, etc.) will be less and that, crucially, the *trainee's professional autonomy* will be what benefits most from these shifts in the preoccupations of the mentoring relationship.

It is extremely hard to avoid *creating overdependence* in trainees if mentors do not make real efforts to scale down their supportive interventions. It is very protective of trainees – and therefore not at all of course a malignant thing – to want to continually be on hand for them, to be a sounding board for lesson ideas, to closely monitor how the challenges of classroom management are being met and so on. Yet, for most practical purposes they will lead a profoundly *un*protected life once qualified and therefore will probably be best prepared for this by a phased reduction in access to a mentor – by mentors 'letting go' in stages.

One of the devices that may prove of assistance in the 'letting go' stage is an extremely straightforward one: it is simply to step up the degree of praise that is being given towards the end of the mentoring relationship. Clearly I cannot advocate providing *unfounded* praise, but wherever possible praising should be a strong element of instilling in trainees the confidence to fit their professional identities as new teachers. The kinds of 'signing off' statements which my own trainees have said were of high value in this context include:

- 'You have a very good grasp of different students' needs. It sometimes takes teachers years to get this …'
- 'I have learnt more from you this year than you have learnt from me.'
- 'You have done your best, far beyond what's expected of you – it's up to the students now.'
- 'You bring a breath of fresh air into teaching and the department as a whole.'
- 'Teaching students with learning difficulties is definitely your calling.'
- '… work your magic.'

References

Ainley, P., and Allen, A. (2009) Regaining the initiative, [Opinion piece] *UC* [the journal of the University and College Union] November.

Cunningham, B. (2004) Some have mentoring thrust upon them: the element of choice in mentoring in PCET environments, *Researching Post-Compulsory Education,* 9/2: 271–82.

DfES (2004) *Equipping our Teachers for the Future: Reforming Initial Teacher Education for the Learning and Skills Sector,* Nottingham: Department for Education and Skills.

Guile, D., and Lucas, N. (1999) Rethinking initial teacher education and professional development in further education: towards the learning professional, in A. Green and N. Lucas (eds), *FE and Lifelong Learning: Realigning the Sector for the Twenty-First Century,* London: Bedford Way Papers.

Healy, C. C., and Welchert, A. J. (1990) Mentoring relations: a definition to advance research and practice, *Educational Researcher*, 19/9: 17–21.

Huberman, M. (1992) Teacher development and instructional mastery, in A. Hargreaves and M. G. Fullan (eds), *Understanding Teacher Development,* New York: Teachers College Press.

Huddleston, P., and Unwin, L. (2007) *Teaching and Learning in Further Education: Diversity and Change* (3rd edn), London: Routledge.

Jackson, P. W. (1992) Helping teachers develop, in A. Hargreaves and M. G. Fullan (eds), *Understanding Teacher Development,* New York: Teachers College Press.

McKelvey, C., and Andrews, J. (1998) Why do they do it? A study into perceptions and motivations of trainee further education lecturers, *Research in Post-Compulsory Education,* 3: 357–67.

West Kent College (n.d.) Mentoring Policy.

Working with colleagues in problem-focused contexts

Chapter objectives

- to review ways in which mentoring may need to incorporate strongly 'remedial' components, and may benefit from collaborative approaches (both formal and informal) in cases of trainees' underperformance.

What I endeavour to do in this chapter is show ways in which, especially where problems are arising over a trainee's progress,[1] collaborating with fellow mentors (and sometimes other key staff) may be advantageous. Arguments – or at least reservations – will obviously present themselves as to the feasibility of such collaboration given the ever-increasing demands being made on mentors' time and energies. Nevertheless, working with others does appear to be an aspect of mentoring which deserves contemplation because of its great potential benefits to both mentors and trainees.

Rationale for working with others

At first sight, mentoring may appear to be an activity solely dependent for its success on a close one-to-one relationship. And the greatest part of the time spent on the task of mentoring a trainee teacher will indeed be spent in this setting. However, where problems are beginning to arise with a trainee there may well be notable advantages to adopting a more collegial approach to these. Where mentors are based in an institution hosting a number of trainees, or employing teachers some of whom are concurrently undergoing training, then in general there will be at least a few staff engaged in mentoring. Teaching can, for much of the time seem – paradoxically – quite a lonely profession, as observed by writers such as Hargreaves and Fullan (1992); it is therefore probably a worthwhile counter to such feelings to engage in the types of collegial working being suggested in this section.

Distributed mentoring

As well as promoting collegiality with other mentors I would also point to the benefits of networking with a wider cross-section of practitioners within a college. The participation which trainees themselves engage in is in reality far more complex than that of their dyadic relationship with their mentor. I am not referring here merely to their relationships with learners, but with their circle of colleagues; some of these may, *de facto*, be functioning as additional mentors, so numerous are their interventions (both supportive and otherwise). This kind of consideration perhaps applies most strongly when we examine the position of full-time trainees, only attending an institution on a teaching practice placement basis. Such trainees very frequently report that they have received valuable guidance from teachers whose classes they have been covering, for example – and often (in the case of specialists such as those in art and design or the sciences) from technicians as well.

The kind of situation described here may equate to the *distributed mentoring* within communities of practice which Pare and LeMaistre (2004) observed. This does not in any way undermine an officially designated mentor's role (although in certain circumstances it is conceivable that it might do so, where certain messages from colleagues relating to aspects of a trainee's practice are at variance with the mentor's). Nor is acknowledging the probability of 'distributed mentoring' existing the same as advocating some kind of 'just ask anyone' culture. A trainee's contact with the kinds of individuals mentioned is more often than not of a type which will only further accelerate their professional learning, and for this reason some mentors may actively promote it. Some trainees will more proactively than others seek out extra support, intuitively identifying colleagues who may be most receptive to requests for additional guidance. From experience, it also appears to be the case that 'distributed mentoring' takes place simply because many college staff are so supportive, and happy to take trainees under their wing; this seems to apply most strongly where such staff perceive that the official mentor is someone with an especially onerous range of responsibilities who is perhaps struggling to meet a trainee's entitlements in terms of regular contact.

Where it is evident to mentors that others have been working supportively with their trainee then it is only sensible to liaise with the individuals concerned. This will allow for more efficient monitoring of the trainee's concerns, and of their developing practice. It will also militate against the possibility of the mixed messages alluded to above, and the needless repetition of points – although of course it is hardly a disaster if a trainee hears important ideas reiterated, and thereby learns that there may in fact be some kind of professional consensus on certain issues.

Opportunities might, though, also present themselves in colleges for the sharing of concerns with others, either informally or formally, with the intention of drawing on a larger potential pool of experience and professional understandings than one mentor alone can hope to possess. There are certainly important issues to bear in mind here, including the very straightforward one concerning time pressures, or finding ourselves to be 'time poor' as it has been sometimes expressed of late. There is obviously going to be a measure of difficulty attached to ever finding good points in the working week when any group of college teachers can come together to discuss matters relating to teacher training.

Clearly, also, it has to be acknowledged that there are potentially serious hazards associated with confidentiality and trust – or rather breaches of these – where trainees, especially those seen as 'underperforming', are being discussed. It is essential, and beneficial to all parties, if mentors who as a group decide to occasionally work together in college to try to solve problems make this fact explicit to trainees, managers and the relevant certificate-awarding institution. Mentors should not involve themselves in any activity that carries the slightest risk that it might be construed by a trainee as 'talking behind their back'. The fact that mentors may meet together as a group to discuss the progress of individual trainees should be out in the open, and the rationale for so doing articulated clearly.

'Action learning sets'

In a number of professional contexts, a valuable framework for professional learning and problem-solving may exist in the form of 'action' learning, and in particular the notion of the 'action learning set'. This will now be briefly outlined, to enable mentors and, perhaps 'non-mentor' colleagues, to decide whether it has the potential to support their work – especially in the context of trainees who are at risk of not succeeding on their programme.

It is possible to critique the proposal that participating in action learning be integrated within any formally *required* dimensions of a mentor's role. The nature of the exercise, and its time demands, means that a number of mentors could well perceive it as entirely unrealistic that they engage with a commitment to an action learning set. However, it seems at least worth indicating what is entailed and what professional benefits may be derived from action learning as a mechanism for linking *reflection* on practice with *action* to improve practice.

A very highly regarded guide to the scope and purposes of action learning in professional settings is that written by Ian McGill and Liz Beaty, first published in 1992. The authors describe:

> a continuous process of learning and reflection, supported by colleagues, with an intention of getting things done. Through action learning individuals learn with and from each other by working on real problems and reflecting on their own experiences.
>
> (McGill and Beaty, 2001: 11)

Working with a group of colleagues, called the 'set', 'the individual … comes to the set to learn from experience and to move on to more effective action' (ibid.). How this process may look in practice can be briefly summarised as follows:

■ A small group – ideally no more than six or seven individuals – will arrange to come together to form a set.

- The set will generate ground rules for its operation, including such matters as length and frequency of meetings, and confidentiality within the set.
- The set members will each bring an issue or concern with which they would value guidance and support.
- Agreement is reached within the set regarding whose issue should be worked on first, and over how many meetings; an allocation of time is agreed on, representing the entitlement (my own term) of each set member.
- The set works in a wholly focused way on the problem presented by one member, enhancing reflection on the nature of the problem, and attempting to arrive at some concrete proposals for action.
- The process of action learning then entails moving on to allow a second set member to present their issue, and benefit from the set's reflections and ideas for action; and so on, over the life of the set.

As will, I hope, be evident, the action learning set is thus a powerful tool for professional learning and action, in that individual set members are able to draw on the insights of others. Sometimes these will perhaps be merely endorsing, and giving legitimacy, to ideas for action the set member may already have been intuitively moving towards, but this in itself can be seen as having high value.

The 'set' is a formal entity, working to clear rules and within stated boundaries. What it ought to be based on, however, are very human, and humanistic, qualities – some of which were alluded to when dealing with mentor attributes much earlier on in this guide. Set members need to experience feelings of mutual professional regard, of trust and of openness. It will not be possible for the set to accomplish much of value if members are guarded about sharing their problems with a trainee because they fear being viewed as in any way inadequate – 'not coping' with their role in teacher training.

Sets work best in an atmosphere of trust where members feel able to disclose their feelings and thoughts to others *without judgement* and in confidence. Lack of trust can render the set impotent as individuals are unlikely to focus on real and important issues where they feel they will be ridiculed or that others will discuss their issue outside the set. (McGill and Beaty, 2001: 54; emphasis added).

Set members need to be able to ask for what they need from the set, and to be able to deal with questioning aimed at getting them to see, or reframe, their particular issue using other perspectives. No issue should be diminished in its importance; if it has been brought to the set it must be approached as meriting serious consideration. In terms of language use within the set, phrases such as 'I just don't see what the problem is' or 'I can't see why you're worrying about it' are highly likely to have negative results, and even to jeopardise the existence of the set. As with the work being carried out with a trainee, a cautious self-monitoring of language use will be well worth striving for.

Certain of the considerations described above, for example the need to try to avoid language use with judgemental overtones, will clearly apply with equal strength to informal relations with other mentors in an institution. The onus on us all to demonstrate consideration and empathy with colleagues who may be experiencing professional challenges is not exclusive to the special nature of action learning sets.

It is, finally, worth alluding to the possibility that working as a set member may be found to be such a positive, empowering, manifestation of collegiality that mentors may actively consider adopting this approach to problem-solving in contexts entirely unrelated to initial teacher training. It may, at the very least, be that the perceived beneficial effects on mentors' interpersonal skills deriving from set membership will be long-lasting ones and that this fact in itself makes having been involved in action learning a positive experience. The way of working in this context potentially arguably has valuable 'spin-offs' into many dimensions of our professional and personal lives:

> Few of us live and work in isolation; so much of our experience in work and life rests upon being effective in the presence of and with other people. Having knowledge about something may be useless if we cannot convey, act, interrelate, in a manner that is effective for the purpose.
>
> (McGill and Beaty, 2001: 118)

It is, therefore, hoped that this extremely brief 'taster' of what action learning may facilitate in the context of problem-focused mentoring might stimulate an exploration of its potential in other areas. A variation on the theme of action learning involves the use of online methods, where mentors may post questions/outline scenarios. Here, what modernity offers is a greater degree of flexibility over the 'where and when' of exchanges between mentors – although perhaps we lose something crucially important in moving away from face-to-face contact?

Liaising with the trainers

Universities will often provide a forum for the sharing both of best practice and difficulties experienced in supporting trainees. However, these will typically be on an extremely occasional basis, even if it is arguable that they should be a far more regular feature of partnership arrangements. Some university-based training schemes simply seem more successful than others at enticing mentors to be actively involved with their in-house events, but here I would only encourage mentors to participate in such advertised events wherever possible. The opportunities to network with mentors from other PCET institutions, and learn something of how mentoring operates across a range of these, is well worthwhile. It is also worth remembering that the agenda for such events is not always that rigid, and some professional 'guerrilla activity' in steering trainers into a focus on the issues which are most exercising mentors may well reap rewards.

Liaising with trainees' tutors

Even where mentors' other commitments preclude actually attending such mentoring-related off-site events as are available, other mechanisms for contact with trainers, and most especially personal tutors, are in place and need to be used.

Whether mentors are working with a full-time or part-time trainee these individuals will have a tutor responsible for their overall progress on their PGCE or CertEd course. This person will often make themselves known at the college/department quite early on, and provide their phone and email contact details. They will be involved, as will mentors, with the observation of trainees' practical teaching and will read mentors (and others') observation and synoptic reports. It is this individual with whom it is absolutely essential to keep in close touch, most especially when it begins to seem as if all is not well with the trainee's performance. 'Performance' is used here, to reiterate this point, as something which can and should be monitored and reported on regarding what is observable both in and outside of a trainee's classes. It will be of equal interest to a tutor to learn about commitment to key aspects of college life such as attending meetings, being present at open evenings and advice sessions, assisting with departmental resources, etc. Clearly trainees who are also college employees will be primarily within the jurisdiction of relevant managers within the organisation, though; in terms of 'taking action' on underperformance in the kinds of areas mentioned here, it will be the college and not the awarding institution (where they are not one and the same) which must decide how to proceed.

One essential point to note in the above contexts is that – how ever inflexible this may appear – there will almost inevitably be requirements placed on mentors to use certain documentation in their correspondence/reporting both to trainees and trainers. It is not at all unheard of, to illustrate this point, for a training institution which wishes to withhold certification from a trainee to be successfully challenged over this purely because an observation report was written on plain paper, rather than an official proforma, and/or where a mentor entered their comments under a set of subheadings which were not 100 per cent aligned with the required ones.

From dyad to triad

Two specific, highly practical ways in which mentors and trainees' tutors can usefully work together are in the, usually related, contexts of

- the three-way meeting with a trainee;
- the co-observation of practical teaching.

In both of these, what occurs is that the normally dyadic relationship between mentor and trainee becomes momentarily a triadic one. The principal advantage of this, as I hope will be made clear, is that of being able to triangulate the views of mentor and tutor, so that the risk of subjective judgements regarding trainee performance is reduced.

For example if both mentor and tutor observe a trainee's class this will simply allow them to compare notes and provide a balanced analysis of a session's strengths and – what is likely to be of more interest if such an event has had to be organised – its weaknesses. Has either the mentor or the tutor adopted an idiosyncratic, overly critical, view of some aspect or aspects of the session, or would both agree that something has indeed been problematic?

The kind of three-way meeting involving mentor, tutor and trainee which I have been involved in has taken the form of either a post-observation *debriefing*, as alluded to above, or a *synoptic review* of progress and problems. Neither of these is an easy event to arrange, given our crowded professional lives, but they almost always have useful outcomes. For instance, trainees' perceptions that 'it's just the mentor/tutor (delete as appropriate) who doesn't like me' can be ameliorated in such a setting if agreement does emerge on the part of both of the responsible individuals that certain areas offer scope for improvement. Sometimes it may even lead trainees to feel that they are seen as being important enough (which is nothing less than the case, of course) to cause two busy professionals to expend extra time and effort on working with them.

On the other hand, having to teach a class with two observers present, rather than just one, is extremely stressful for some trainees – and may even pull down their performance further. And the experience of the three-way meeting may feel to a trainee like being 'ganged up on'. Both situations need especially skilful presentation and handling; the *rationale* for both needs to be made exceptionally clear, and the potentially positive benefits need to be stressed. The key mentor – and trainer – attribute of being able to empathise will come to the fore, alongside the management of such practicalities as setting up unthreatening room arrangements as far as the three-way meeting is concerned.

References

Hargreaves, A., and Fullan, M. (1992) *Understanding Teacher Development*, New York: Teachers College Press.

McGill, I., and Beaty, L. (2001) *Action Learning: A Guide for Professional, Management and Educational Development* (2nd edn), London: Kogan Page.

Pare, A., and LeMaistre, C. (2004) Learning through complex participation: distributed mentoring in communities of practice, in P. Tynjala, J. Valiman and G. Boulton-Lewis (eds), *Higher Education and Working Life: Collaborations, Confrontations and Challenges,* Amsterdam: Elsevier.

Case studies and critical incidents in mentoring

Chapter objectives

■ to examine the merits of two discrete, but clearly interrelated, perspectives on professional learning, focusing on their role within mentoring.

Case studies in mentoring

> The tendency to promote stories of happy endings is hardly surprising, for who would wish (or dare) to wash any dirty linen about unproductive or failed relationships in public, let alone define such failures as mentoring?
>
> (Colley, 2003)

Helen Colley was no doubt correct in pointing to the way in which the benefits – the positive outcomes – of the activity of mentoring are those that tend to be accentuated and celebrated. It would be dispiriting in the extreme to spend any significant amount of time dissecting ways in which mentoring relationships may fail, and my own preoccupation in this guide has been to try to promote and celebrate the value of mentors' work. Nevertheless, it seems both worthwhile and realistic to at least include some references in what follows to less successful mentoring relationships – by way of 'cautionary tales', and with an exceptionally high degree of anonymisation having been an overriding concern when depicting them. The main emphasis of the first section of the chapter is indeed, though, to illustrate how Colley's 'happy endings' have been arrived at.

The three case studies that follow are presented in the form of first-person 'testimonies', having been supplied (mostly) by recently qualified new entrants. Each of the trainees who agreed to contribute the case studies followed a full-time, pre-service PGCE course, so none were employed by a PCET institution while being mentored.

I have only amended originals in any way where I judged there was a serious risk of either the trainee or the mentors being identifiable. Following each case study I have indicated what some of the key issues – both positive and negative – appear to be, although I am aware that some readers might perhaps judge this to have been superfluous.

Case study one

What follows seems to offer an especially interesting case study, in that the author – a quite outstanding teacher, even as a trainee – has subsequently herself become a highly effective teacher trainer.

While I was doing my PGCE, I read a book on mentoring, and although I don't remember much about it I do remember that the author recommended that mentors should spend 70 minutes a week with their student teachers. The reason why this figure stuck in my mind was because it seemed such a huge length of time, given that I spent on average (over the year) about a couple of minutes a week with my mentor.

According to The Institute my mentor was supposed to guide and to instruct me in terms of college administration, health and safety, and pastoral aspects of education; she was supposed to inform me about the curriculum, the students and their work, about issues of classroom management and so on. However, my mentor didn't seem to have read the guidebook on effective mentoring, or if she had, she had taken to heart the bit about not being overprotective.

At the start I saw her quite regularly, as she arranged which lessons I should observe. After the first week, however, I was left to take the initiative and to approach teachers so that I could watch a variety of lessons (from Key Skills to A Level), and more importantly, perhaps, a range of teaching styles, methods and strategies.

It didn't seem long after that that I was being approached to cover lessons. One instance I remember vividly was where a teacher had been to New York over the half-term break and quite clearly couldn't face teaching first thing on Monday morning. There was clearly no supervision going on here and at no point did I ever teach with another teacher in the room. Being a relatively experienced teacher, I didn't mind this too much, but what I *would* have liked was some time to talk about teaching strategies with her (about successful methods she had used to teach a particular class/student/ text; about effective teaching strategies and activities that she had seen other teachers use, etc.).

What she *did* do was to plan my initial observations of other teachers (albeit for a brief period); she did organise my teaching timetable (although this became increasingly ad hoc), and we did have a couple of planned meetings during the year (these were generally strategic sessions in which we discussed my timetable).

Therefore, while her planning, liaising, and guiding may have been somewhat lacking, and she clearly believed in the hit-and-miss, pick-it-up-as-you-go-along style of mentoring, in terms of teaching she did lead by example. She was a good teacher, with an excellent classroom manner and with finely honed classroom management skills. In her observation of my lesson, too, she was thorough and constructive.

In retrospect, I can see that the reason for her 'hands-off' approach to mentoring was not that she had no regard for the post or for me. The reasons were more complicated than this. I suspect that I did not ask enough of her, and was flattered to think that she felt I was sufficiently competent take the initiative, to plan and to run classes myself. I also think that her incentive for being a dedicated mentor seemed to have shrunk to the fact that she could put it on her CV. A good mentor lies partly in a successful relationship between the university, the college and the teacher him/herself. If the support is lacking from either the university or the college, the teacher's motivation has to be intrinsic. The college at which I worked received money for each student teacher that they took on, but none of that money seemed to be translated into either pay or relief hours for the mentors. If I had known that relief hours had been awarded to my mentor, the whole system of meeting, planning, etc. could have been more structured, with an allotted discussion time set for each week.

In the years following my PGCE I have mentored many student teachers. It has only been by doing this that I have discovered just how many different roles and jobs a successful mentor has, and just how difficult (without relief hours) it is to find 70 minutes a week in a busy teaching timetable.

Commentary

This account teaches us a good deal, beginning with the way in which the trainee had discerned that a guidance handbook supplied to the mentor had not been read. But there is, of course, a real awareness, gained through subsequent mentoring/training, of the challenges caused by an individual having insufficient time to mentor. How practitioners ought to respond to this professional dilemma can never be legislated for; it is one, however, where the existence within an institution of an experienced 'lead mentor' (Tang-Wong, 2011), able to 'mentor the mentors', would be of great potential value.

Case study two

By way of providing a much different perspective on the experience of being mentored, one which was, at times, so demotivating as to have almost caused the trainee to withdraw from her programme, this contains some important lessons for us.

When I began my PGCE in September 2003 I was hopeful for the future and excited and full of enthusiasm to start my teaching placement practice, which would hopefully lead me further towards the change of career which I had chosen for myself. I enjoyed the first two weeks of the course at my training college, and was not put off too greatly by the course work or the academic demands of the course for the coming months; and although nervous, I was hopeful that I would come to enjoy or at least relish the challenges that my placement would present. Although I didn't feel quite as confident about my teaching skills in practice, I was hopeful that with support and guidance from my mentor along the way, I would soon be able to develop the skills necessary to be able to teach effectively in the classroom environment, and build on any existing skills I had acquired in previous teaching roles within the caring professions where I had nearly twenty years of previous working experience.

Eventually I heard from the college and was given a contact name for my mentor; but despite my efforts to contact him, I did not eventually get to meet my mentor until the placement started, during one of our induction sessions in the training section of the college. I met him briefly and we arranged to meet the next week when the placement started officially. When we did meet the following week it was very briefly and although I suggested having regular meetings during the placement for progress updates, and these were agreed to, in the end only the minimum number of meetings were eventually held throughout the placement.

I was invited to attend only one of my mentor's lessons during the first term to observe prior to starting my own teaching practice, and very few other teachers at the college seemed willing to be observed within my department, although there were a few exceptions to whom I am most appreciative, but they did not include my mentor. He did not attend or observe any of my taught lessons at all during my first term, and I generally had fleeting glimpses of him throughout the whole placement, when he would dash in and out of the staffroom between lessons or meetings, ask if I was ok, and then dash out of the room again, barely stopping long enough to hear my reply.

It seemed that my mentor found out about my progress by asking other staff how I was coping, he never once came to see me teach a class himself until the middle of the second term of the placement, and gave me no feedback at all on my teaching practice until *AFTER* my first observed assessment, which he failed to conduct himself, asking the placement co-ordinator to observe in his place. After the feedback from this, I felt very disappointed and humiliated by the whole experience, since this was the first proper feedback I had received on my teaching practice since the start of the placement; and I was very angry, particularly with my mentor, that I had got to the second term of my placement and neither he nor anyone else had spoken to me prior to this time about there having been any problems with either my teaching methods or my classroom management abilities; so that I had no way of knowing until that stage that there were aspects of my teaching style which in the college's view were unsatisfactory.

I knew I was not the most experienced teacher in the classroom and therefore was keen to have regular progress reports and welcomed any constructive criticism of my performance in class; but I did spend time planning my lessons meticulously and had shown the lesson plans to the subject tutor as well as to my mentor, who had had plenty of opportunity to advise me of any problems if necessary prior to either of my placement or training college observed assessments, but had failed to.

I felt very much as if I had been set up to fail by the staff at my placement college and particularly by my mentor. I had some quite challenging classes to teach during my placement and eventually, toward the middle of the spring term, after finally deciding I no longer had any confidence in my mentor, I decided to consult my personal tutor about my concerns regarding my progress on the placement and the absence of support and advice from my mentor. Following his intervention and a three-way meeting with the college placement co-ordinator, I went away for the Easter break feeling a little more reassured and hopeful that things would improve for the final term of the placement.

In the final term I returned to the college determined to finish the placement as best I could and complete all the required teaching hours and reports that were required of me to satisfy my training college and hopefully to complete my final observed assessment with a reasonable grade. Fortunately I managed to achieve all these things by the end of the placement.

But I left my placement college feeling that my confidence in myself as a newly qualified teacher had been badly undermined by my experiences there. That I hadn't been given a very well balanced insight into what classroom teaching involved, and disappointed that I had not been given a chance to grow and develop the skills as a beginner teacher in the way that I had hoped I would be able to do at the beginning of the course. Mostly I felt saddened and disappointed that I seemed to have lost some confidence, and some of the optimism and enthusiasm for teaching that I had started the course with; and on reflection since my course ended, can only conclude that the reason for this was entirely related to the lack of effective mentoring provided by my placement college during my training.

Commentary

This somewhat dispiriting testimony truly underscores how the crucial importance of effective mentoring is probably best proven where it has *not* been the experience of the trainee. With considerable attention on my own part being paid to salvaging something of the trainee's self-confidence, she was however subsequently able to contemplate applying for teaching positions. A number of negatives appear to have come into play here, including the fact the mentor had delegated the observation of an important, formally assessed, session without the trainee having been made aware of the reasons.

Case study three

The third and final case study returns us to a far more positive situation, one seeing the appointment of the trainee concerned to the curriculum department of their college in which they had completed their placement.

I didn't have a huge amount of expectations to begin with, and wasn't entirely sure what exactly to expect from a mentor. I suppose I naively hoped for someone who would explain the dos and don'ts of teaching, alongside an idea of the college rules; someone who would be a link between the PGCE and the placement college.

In sight of this particular expectation, I also didn't think that a mentor would have teaching commitments. I had hoped for someone who would provide me with perfect textbook answers to my questions, while reinforcing the content of the PGCE. I also hoped for compassion and support.

What I got was far better than all that; my mentor gave me an optimistic yet realistic insight into teaching, consistent support, while providing encouragement and valuable feedback regarding my teaching practice.

I wasn't patronised and made to feel like the 'inadequate student teacher' that needs to learn everything. Instead my existing subject knowledge was brought onto courses, and I was encouraged to use what I know in innovative and creative ways in the classroom. I was taken on as 'the production person' in the department.

Praise was given, as well as constructive criticism, and a well-balanced approach towards my progress prompted me to address all feedback. Motivation was provided through different methods, such as allowing me to integrate subject areas that I was particularly interested in into lessons/handouts.

Ideas that worked were openly praised, reused and borrowed by other teachers in the department, making me feel like a valued and appreciated member of the team.

My mentor always had time for me, even if her own workload was ridiculously high. She had provided me with her contact details and I was able to contact her at home if there were any issues I was particularly worried about or wanted to discuss.

We also had regular meeting slots in which we discussed my feelings regarding progress so far, concerns, etc. If I had nothing to discuss in relation to this, then we would lesson-plan or discuss handout designs for future sessions. The meetings used to last 20-40 minutes and I found them immensely useful.

If I made a mess of things or had a particularly horrible lesson, I was initially supported and provided with a positive spin on the situation. The situation was then later discussed when things had cooled down, or I had things in more perspective, and constructive criticism alongside effective strategies to explore were discussed. I found this approach sensitive, both boosting morale and motivation while allowing me to address the issue(s).

My mentor really mentored me. I know that sounds silly, but she really provided an immense level of support. And this support was consistent for the duration of my placement.

Commentary

This account contains a number of interesting observations, but one of the most interesting seems to concern the steps that were taken by the mentor to *integrate* the trainee – a clear role is found for her in the department which both purposefully exploits her existing skills, to the department's benefit, and boosts her confidence; she is moving from the periphery to a far more central position, even though she is not actually employed in the institution in question. Another key dimension of the relationship between trainee and mentor is that there appears to have been an especially non-judgmental, non-censorious attitude on the part of the latter when things didn't go well – even when they were 'horrible'. Alternative strategies are presented by the mentor as ones *'to explore'*, not ones that were henceforth to be used instead of 'unsuccessful' ones. There are, in brief, a number of illustrations in this last case study of the ways in which the dialogue between trainee and mentor constitutes a genuine *'learning conversation'* (Carnell *et al.*, 2006), albeit one necessarily punctuated by the mentor having to deal with her own 'ridiculously high' teaching load!

Some concluding points

All three of the above self-narratives appear to emphasise certain aspects of what mentors need to be aware of as they begin to work with a trainee. To select merely a few 'lessons' from the case studies, they might be:

- Trainees usually come to the relationship with both *expectations* and *misconceptions*: 'I didn't think that a mentor would have teaching commitments …'.
- The extremely high value placed by trainees on criticism needing to be *constructive* in nature.
- The positive results of building on trainees' *prior experiences*, and the negative results of failing to do so (the self-esteem of a trainee who had had teaching roles within the caring profession that she had worked in for twenty years would almost certainly have been enhanced had this fact been drawn on).
- There is a highly desirable *balance* that needs to be struck between being 'hands off' and 'interventionist' – the latter mode pointing to the need, for instance, to actually observe a trainee's teaching, even if only on a purely informal basis, at a relatively early stage in the mentoring relationship.

I would want to propose that, incidentally, one of the various ways in which mentors might be able to demonstrate compliance with the present '30 hours' rule (engaging with CPD activities for this amount of time, annually) would be by documenting (anonymised) case studies of helping trainee teachers; where such case studies include concrete examples of improvements in trainee – or mentor, for that matter – practice they would be especially worthwhile.

Critical incidents in mentoring

A critical incident can be viewed as an event in one's professional life which has special significance for one or more reasons. For example:

- it may have involved being unprepared, to a very unsettling degree, to deal with a problem which arose;
- it caused a disturbance of equilibrium;
- it took the form of a dilemma, ethical or otherwise;
- it can be seen to have led to a lasting change in professional behaviour, principles or perceptions;
- it has caused continuing reflections over a substantial period – one keeps revisiting the incident, seeing more of its nature and implications on each occasion when its details are recalled;
- it may have had major practical outcomes (including, for example, entering, or leaving, the teaching profession).

Critical incidents as a component of professional learning are being used analytically within fields such as medicine, nursing and social work. The 'life or death' nature of many of the professional decisions made in such occupations could probably be cited by way of explanation for their adoption of critical incidents as a tool (Cunningham, 2008). But teachers, too, must make numerous decisions of importance in each working day, and are responsible – usually in teams – for the development and successes of their learners. And when things go seriously wrong in classrooms the lasting effects of this may well also have long-term – perhaps even lifelong – consequences. For these kinds of reasons we have witnessed relatively recently the incorporation into the assessment frameworks of many PCET training programmes of an assignment (an example of which is provided as Appendix 1) calling for trainees to describe and interrogate the nature of a critical incident that they have experienced; such assignments most typically ask that trainees focus in particular on how the incident has deepened their understanding of learning and teaching, and has played a part in enhancing their practice.

It is hoped therefore that mentors will find something of value in a brief examination of the nature of critical incidents. It is possible to apply the idea to (a) the early professional development of mentored trainees (in particular their growing understanding of the nature of effective teaching) and (b) the continuing professional learning, about mentoring, of mentors themselves. David Tripp's (1993) book *Critical Incidents in Teaching* is a key resource for mentors who would like to explore this area in more depth – but is strongly rooted in the systems and cultures of schools rather than colleges. Mentors skilfully engaging in discussions of critical incidents with trainees and also openly discussing their own critical incidents with peers will undoubtedly be extending both their trainees' and their own repertoire of mentoring skills.

A valuable starting point is for mentors, having gained a basic understanding themselves of what is involved in critical incident analysis, to induct trainees into the benefits of this approach to reflective practice. Key points will be to ensure trainees appreciate:

- that, almost by definition, not all incidents can possibly be critical;
- that the 'criticality' of an incident may not be immediately evident – in general a period of reflection will be needed before its status as such can be discerned;
- that there is a range of possible settings in which critical incidents can be experienced – a classroom's walls are not what limits the potential for critical incidents to occur;
- that while negativity – e.g. stress, hurt feelings or anger – may often characterise an incident, its underlying nature can ultimately be positive in terms of its influence on professional development.

Virtually all teacher trainees, whether on pre- or in-service programmes, have been required for some time now to maintain *reflective logs or journals*; unless a training provider explicitly bars such a modification, mentors could encourage their trainees to include a section specifically titled 'Critical Incident Log'. Entries in this can be discussed in mentor–trainee meetings, or where a group of trainees is based in an institution they could be shared within the wider forum which is thus possible. Critical Incident Workshops can even be organised, to allow for the fullest possible exploration of any key professional themes which emerge from trainees' experiences.

There are of course risks associated with adopting a 'critical incidents' framework in the mentoring of early career professionals. One of these is, to reiterate the point, that *not* all incidents can possibly be critical. On a week by week basis, trainees will be experiencing a great number of professional interactions with learners, colleagues, support staff and mentors and in reality very few of these indeed will have an enormous impact on their practice. At the end of a term, however, it might well be that some of this interaction can be seen to have a larger significance – and one or two elements might indeed possess a criticality in terms of how they have sharpened the reflective process, or are actually triggering a change in practice. Similarly, not all the mistakes made by a trainee in their classes will be that unsettling (for either learners or trainees themselves) and the professional learning stimulated by such mistakes will be of significance only at the microscale. For example, it may be embarrassing for someone to realise they have inadvertently collated some pages of a handout in the incorrect order – this may get a laugh, perhaps, from a group – but it is not indicative of any major failure to understand the purpose of employing such an essential aid to learning.

By contrast, however, a trainee might be approached by a learner group's representative(s) with a complaint that their teaching seems to largely comprise talking to – usually far too many – PowerPoint slides. This *is* the type of exchange – especially if it is clear that it deals with an issue that has apparently been festering for some time – that will, or ought to, cause very serious, critical, reflection on how the job of classroom teaching has been being approached. *Why* has the trainee been using one method in preference to all others? Have the merits of variation of approach not been adequately considered? And what has been going so wrong in the relationship with a learner group that such a crucially important piece of feedback has not been given much earlier? For all these reasons – and probably others that readers will conceive of – there appears to be a *critical* dimension here to what the trainee has been on the receiving end of.

The second important risk attached to the use of critical incidents with trainees is that the construct can be accused (as reflective practice itself sometimes is) of being too backward-looking, fruitlessly introspective and limiting. The phrase 'navel-gazing' is one often used by critics of reflection in professional development – and perhaps sometimes this harsh perspective may have been justified. Yet the whole point of critical incidents – and here we might usefully recourse to the *OED* – is that they mark 'a point at which some action, property or condition *passes over into another*' (my emphasis). In other words, it is the *transformational* potential of critical incidents to which attention needs to be drawn – they allow a focus on the 'before', but far more importantly cause us to look towards the 'after'. If we have accepted a claim for mentoring as being a *transformative* set of actions, as well as simply supportive ones, a corollary is that it becomes much easier to acknowledge and celebrate the developmental nature of reflection in general and critical incidents in particular.

TABLE 7.1 Settings where there is the potential for critical incidents to occur

1.	Another teacher's classroom (possibly the mentor's), in which a trainee is conducting an observation
2.	The debriefing room, when discussing with a mentor a recent observation
3.	The staffroom, where colleagues' attitudes and perceptions may be displayed
4.	At a meeting with learners' parents
5.	At an 'open advice' session for prospective students, where their aspirations and preconceptions regarding college life can be discerned
6.	Socially, when networking informally with other trainees

It is, as indicated, important however to raise trainees' awareness of the great diversity of settings in which the origins of critical incidents may lie. Some examples of such settings, besides classrooms, are given in Table 7.1.

Why it is helpful for mentors to underline the broad range of settings/circumstances in which critical incidents may be experienced is that there is some evidence that trainees may otherwise become somewhat fixated on the idea that they relate almost exclusively to confrontation in classrooms. In fact, a 'revelatory' observation from someone else's classroom (item 1 in Table 7.1) can represent a critical incident – for example, an aspect of the practice which has been observed can lead to a fundamental rethinking of the trainee's own. Feedback given in an observation (item 2) may include a hugely important piece of much-needed confidence building; this can happen when a trainee's self-perception of their performance to date has been extremely negative, and overly self-critical – they have been undermining themselves. A mentor providing a degree of balance in this sort of situation is able, *critically*, to move things on by using words to the effect of 'no, it wasn't anywhere near as bad as you think – actually you're being far, far too hard on yourself'.

References

Carnell, E., MacDonald, J., and Askew, S. (2006) *Coaching and Mentoring in Higher Education: A Learning-Centred Approach*, London: University of London, Institute of Education.

Colley, H. (2003) *Mentoring for Social Inclusion: A Critical Approach to Nurturing Mentor Relationships*, London: RoutledgeFalmer.

Cunningham, B. (2008) Critical incidents in professional life and learning, in B. Cunningham (ed.), *Exploring Professionalism*, London: Bedford Way Papers, pp. 161–89.

Tang-Wong, J. (2011) [A Study] To assess the feasibility of constructing 'Developmental Relationships' as a relevant mentoring model for the Diploma in Business and Social Enterprise [at the Ngee Ann Polytechnic of Singapore], unpublished EdD thesis, Institute of Education, University of London.

Tripp, D. (1993) *Critical Incidents in Teaching*, London: Routledge.

Mentors' continuing professional development

I have found mentoring an enriching experience from which I have gained a deeper understanding of teaching.

> (Anon, 2010 – comment from evaluation exercise
> conducted at the end of a year of mentors'
> involvement with a training programme)

In this short chapter I aim to focus on ways in which the effective, forward-looking, mentor can build on their experiences by weaving them into their own personal 'professional projects', their plans to progress. Such 'projects' are, for example, being formally promoted in some colleges through the vehicle of the *personal development plans* (PDPs) which staff may use as the basis for their appraisals and in connection with other institutional processes relating to human resources.

It seems wholly appropriate that involvement in the role of mentor is seen as a part of mentors' own continuing professional development. This is not only meant to refer to the positive benefits accruing to currently held teaching skills from observing and engaging in dialogue with trainees (as illustrated by the quotation above). It relates more to the ways in which mentors may actively exploit their experiences when seeking professional advancement, either within their present institution or elsewhere. In a number of respects, especially as the profile of mentoring continues to be raised in professional life, the kinds of skills mentors will have used are extremely likely to be viewed as high-level ones, of value in responsible positions. They are, therefore, eminently *transferable* ones.

From certain perspectives, it may even emerge that the ability and willingness to engage in mentoring becomes an *essential*, rather than merely *desirable*, criterion for the majority of substantial posts in the PCET sector – in other words, one of the basic minimum requirements for appointment as a full-time, established teacher who has completed a post-qualifying year. Writing in the context of teachers/ mentors delivering Skills for Life programmes, Jay Derrick for example airs the view that 'Mentoring must become a normal part of all experienced teachers' job roles' (Derrick, 2004: 25). Interestingly, though, this writer adds the important observation that 'infrastructure needs to exist in all regions for training, supporting and quality assuring mentors' (ibid.). This would appear to further extend, regionally, the notion of an appropriate institutional architecture for mentoring being proposed in Chapter 1.

As a starting point for the creation of an *inventory* of skills and attributes to which attention can be drawn in applications which are being made for posts it is, quite simply, perfectly legitimate to describe the degree of respect, and status, already accorded to an individual when they have been designated as a mentor. Although we can probably all think of instances where appointments to the mentor role have resulted from the 'no one else available' syndrome, these will be very rare. In general selection panels will almost certainly work on the assumption that mentors will have been given the responsibilities attached to the work for a mixture of the following reasons:

- relatively long service in an institution, or at the least a degree of 'loyalty' to it and a history of positive interaction with colleagues and superiors;
- evidence of skills in the area of self-organisation, and the management of course documentation;
- high-level classroom teaching skills, which are also in a number of ways susceptible to objective measures – for instance, gradings awarded in internal or external inspection exercises, or evaluative comments supplied by college learners;
- reliability, and perhaps the kind of willingness and flexibility attached to covering for absent colleagues – in a nutshell, a track record of taking on more than has strictly speaking been required of one in a post;
- somewhat less easily quantified, hard to pin down, attributes (or 'dispositions') – but vital ones – such as the 'personal impact and presence', discussed earlier in connection with the observation of practical teaching (Chapter 4).

Many of us are naturally reticent about making too many claims regarding our strengths – blowing our own trumpets – but the kinds of people skills and organisational skills routinely deployed by practising mentors are clearly very sought-after ones. This applies not only in respect of posts in the broad areas of education and training (including teacher training, of course) but in related professional realms – if that is where our career aspirations happen to be leading us. It would, moreover, be feasible to supply evidence to substantiate the strengths to which one wishes to draw attention; for instance a record of the number of trainees successfully completing their programmes over a period of time, with a mentor's support.

Mentoring skills are, then, transferable ones, and in some ways are fairly clearly related to *management*, in its broadest sense – mentors have managed individual trainees' timetables (those on full-time, pre-service courses), effectively liaised with colleagues in compiling these, managed observations of classroom practice, structured debriefings following these, and taken on a 'troubleshooting' role when things have not all been as they should be. And *coaching*, an increasingly acknowledged and valued dimension of mentoring (or at least adjunct to it) is another function which could be listed here. It is probably self-evident that these kinds of tasks are not at all dissimilar to those performed regularly by curriculum managers, and as such will in general be seen as constituting a useful preparation for such positions.

Furthermore, mentors will have written detailed formative and summative reports, been involved in target-setting, and very possibly counselled trainees regarding career pathways in the PCET sector. All of these dimensions of being a mentor are well worth celebrating in applications, always being cautious not to dwell too much on the kinds of things referred to here at the expense of issues perhaps more strongly linked with specific sets of selection criteria. Good mentors have invested a great deal of their time, thought and energy to the induction and ongoing support of trainees, and it is entirely legitimate that such an investment might have somewhat longer term professional rewards as well as those deriving from the day-to-day contact with trainees.

Some of the above ideas were some time ago woven into an interesting statement comprising 'recommendations for mentors' to be found in the collaborative *Mentoring towards Excellence* (FENTO/AoC, 2001). This report described the 'learning conversations about mentoring' held in twenty-nine colleges in connection with this publication, and which gave rise to the list in Table 8.1. Although some of the individual items read more like recommendations for college managers – or even

TABLE 8.1 Recommendations for mentors

• Mentoring should be developed and promoted as a supportive and developmental process.
• The mentors should have job descriptions that clarify their role.
• Mentoring and observation should apply to all teachers: full time; part time; supply and agency teachers.
• Mentoring should be part of the management's commitment to improving quality and raising standards of teaching and learning.
• Mentors should be best-practice practitioners.
• Teaching observations should be used to identify 'grade 1' teachers who are strong role models to become mentors.
• Mentors should be formally trained.
• Mentors should be either paid for mentoring, or be given time to carry out the job.
• Mentoring should be used to increase the sharing of good practice.
• A mentor needs to be a successful practitioner with strong interpersonal skills.

Source: FENTO/AoC, 2001: 8.

policy-makers – the list is notable for being an authoritative indication of what is almost certainly still current thinking in at least some key PCET institutions.

If such a collation of points from the 'learning conversations' forming the empirical basis for the report were to gain a wide currency it could usefully serve to underscore the centrality of mentors' high standing in colleges, and thereby their suitability for further professional advancement.

Mentoring as a dimension of CPD

It has become a commonplace that in any professional area there is now a need to demonstrate a readiness to continually refine and extend our skills. But in certain ways we may still have a somewhat blinkered view of what exactly can legitimately be described as 'professional development'. As Graham Guest has expressed it:

> It is easy to assume that CPD is just a matter of attending training courses off the job. This is certainly one aspect, but there are many more. CPD activities can include on-the-job training, open learning, short courses, conferences, seminars, workshops, self-study, preparing and making presentations and *being a coach or mentor*.
>
> (Guest, 2004: 22; emphasis added)

From what we have seen of the demands of effective mentoring, and the range of skills which mentors must display, there is clearly much more professional development attached to the successful practice of the activity than would result from choosing, say, to remain 'purely' a classroom teacher (although this is, of course, not intended as a statement to in any way diminish the value of professional accomplishments in the classroom). Alongside this fact, it is indisputable that mentoring in the post-compulsory sector has been accorded even greater value in the context of the reforms to the training of new entrants to teaching within it. Therefore there is evidently much to be gained by mentors who can navigate the various possibilities for celebrating what they have achieved – for themselves as well as for the trainees with whom they have worked.

One possible way in which mentoring activities might be documented might well be as part of a Personal Development Record (or Plan) (PDR/P). In fact, such a record 'may well soon become the norm, supplementing our online CVs and personal websites' (ibid.). The PDR could be organised in such a way as to highlight the *transferability* of the professional learning which has accrued from mentoring, and, specifically, to indicate ways in which it has better equipped an individual for increased managerial responsibilities.

Not only mentoring itself, but participating in mentoring-related activities is worthy of recognition as CPD. To link together two of the possibilities referred to by Guest (namely, mentoring and preparing a presentation) it might be feasible to contribute to an organised event where the focus is best practice in mentoring; a number of practising mentors have now done so at seminars organised at the writer's base institution over the years, adding greatly to the credibility of the programmes that have been offered.

However, if these kinds of considerations appear somewhat too instrumental, then it is probably necessary to reattach this discussion to mentors' more immediate concerns, and focus on ways in which improvements to current practice can be sought. Some ideas of relevance to this end are presented below.

Improving the quality of one's mentoring

The ability to mentor effectively is susceptible to a range of quantitative and qualitative measures, some of these being:

- in an institution having in place transparent mechanisms for identifying staff to join a mentoring team, the very fact of having been selected for the role;
- successful completion by trainees of their programmes;
- evaluations completed by such trainees;
- comments supplied, informally or formally, by withdrawing (perhaps even complaining) trainees.

The evolution of one's mentoring skills will occur as a result of using them regularly – the 'practice makes perfect' effect. But other positive effects can be derived from such activities as attending events with a 'sharing of best practice' focus, and (even better) contributing to the design and delivery of these. Actively evaluating one's own practice is, however, to be commended even more highly; it is, then, worth giving some thought to how best to undertake this evaluation. Let us therefore try to expand on the third point in the listing beginning this section.

'Group' evaluation exercises might be conducted where a number of trainees in one institution are asked to respond anonymously to written questions posed regarding the quality of mentoring they have received over a period. Each member of a team of mentors can examine and discuss the picture of mentoring which emerges, and make educated guesses concerning which evaluative comments (positive or negative) might apply to their own efforts. This sort of strategy is liable to provide a useful overview, but is probably too blunt an instrument for most individual mentors' liking if they wish to glean a greater degree of insight into how their own performance has been perceived.

The use of focus groups is worth considering, where trainees can discuss their experiences with mentors. Ideally, such a forum would be one in which the distorting effects of power relations are minimised, and one way of tackling this issue is simply by making sure that neither 'side' feels outnumbered. Aim, therefore, for as even a balance between mentors or trainees as can be engineered. Alternatively, where a focus group can be facilitated by a neutral third party, perhaps a college's staff development manager (although admittedly here 'neutrality' is questionable), this allows for a higher degree of comfort.

The above devices have obvious, quite severe, limitations when it comes to eliciting evaluations of an individual mentor's performance. To obtain such an evaluation will be contingent on the trainees involved forfeiting their anonymity and it must therefore be acknowledged to be a process which will generally only produce any reliable results where the mentor–trainee relationship has been an overwhelmingly positive one. It probably takes a relatively courageous trainee to offer honest feedback if this is negative. On the other hand, actually posing the difficult questions in the first place probably also calls for a measure of courage. As with so many other aspects of mentoring practice, the well-judged and skilful use of language in posing appropriate questions (in this specific context reassurance of 'no reprisals' being the obvious priority) will be a real asset to the mentor concerned.

Mentors' support for trainees is usually evaluated by training institutions, and more often than not there would be no obstacles presented to mentors actively seeking out how they have fared in such exercises. Again, however, training institutions would in general need a high degree of reassurance should seriously negative issues have been raised by a trainee – and on ethical grounds might in some instances not actually feel able to relay the contents of particular evaluations. Where such a response is encountered, it only makes sense to ask for the assistance of the training provider in strongly encouraging a trainee to feel secure in raising even critical issues directly with their mentor/former mentor. It is virtually impossible to improve one's performance where the deficiencies are only being guessed at. But the summative evaluations, i.e. those carried out at the end of a trainee's programme, while they do not positively contribute to ongoing mentoring relationships, can profoundly influence the nature and effectiveness of future ones.

Accreditation for mentoring

This possibility has been touched on earlier, in the Introduction to this book, when dealing with some elements of the raised status of mentoring. Here we can perhaps merely reiterate that opportunities do exist at a number of universities to gain credit for the high-level work-based professional learning for which mentoring provides evidence. Programmes are typically at master's ('M') level and successful completion of these is usually via a mix of portfolio assessment and extended writing (some of which will typically call for a deeper exploration of the kinds of theoretical models alluded to in Chapter 3). Oxford Brookes University's MA in Coaching and Mentoring Practice is of interest, for example, as are programmes run at a number of other institutions including Middlesex University, Anglia University and the Institute of Education. One of the most positive aspects about such possibilities is that there generally exist in such HEIs as these options for Accreditation of Prior Experiential Learning (APEL) against relevant criteria.

Employers in the PCET sector may be amenable to helping with the registration and other costs attached to these sorts of studies. The key to successful applications for such assistance seems to be being able to make a credible claim for the ways in which mentors see that their own professional practice, and teaching quality within an institution, can be enhanced by following one of the programmes. Clearly, however, the source of most relevant advice in this connection will be the senior individual within a college with staff development or human resources responsibilities.

Research and writing

At the outset I would need to acknowledge that a number of practising mentors will already possess a pedigree as published authors, especially in the realm of subject-specific texts. Here I will, however, focus on research and writing which might stem from the activity of mentoring itself. As well as seeking opportunities to document their own professional practice, and to share it with others – perhaps those newer to mentoring – with a view to possible career development, it is also often likely to be true that mentors' *academic* skills have further potential to be both refined and celebrated. Probably one of the most realistic, constructive and purposeful ways in which this might be accomplished is by engaging in research activity focusing on mentoring. A great deal of professional learning is actually taking place during mentoring relationships – sometimes the same kind of 'trial and error learning' which ordinarily teaching might be said to entail.

Such learning can be viewed as leading to 'really useful knowledge'; the 'outcomes' of the learning are fairly immediately used to inform one's own professional practice, and/or perhaps that of colleagues. In this sense we are almost on the verge of being able to claim we are in the realm of action research. Such an approach is a highly appropriate one where 'the effects of a specific intervention are to be evaluated' (Cohen *et al.*, 2000: 73). The 'intervention' in the present context would of course be the activity of mentoring.

A range of academic and professional journals would be receptive to individual or collaboratively written articles which focus on mentoring, including for example:

- *Research in Post-Compulsory Education*
- *Journal of Vocational Education and Training*
- *Journal of Further and Higher Education*
- *Teacher Development*
- *International Journal of Mentoring and Coaching.*

It is perhaps easy to be daunted by various aspects of writing for publication (not least by the prospect of trying to carve out in one's professional life sufficient time in which to get involved in the activity). However, many journals, including most of those above, have a strong *practitioner* focus, i.e. they are more concerned with case studies and action research projects (especially where improvements in quality can be evidenced as a result of the project) than with highly theoretical work. It is true, though, that there is a kind of 'pecking order' of journals within the academic world, and the publications deemed to be most prestigious will often reject material they do not judge to be 'weighty' enough in terms of its theoretical components.

Beyond giving the obvious advice that it is therefore a good starting point to research the nature of the 'typical' article being accepted by any given journal, and its place in the status hierarchy of published academic writing, there are probably certain other key points (both positive and negative) to bear in mind:

- For the most strongly competed-for posts, being able to provide even a fairly brief publications record could be a distinctive feature of an application. All other things being equal, such an addition to an application could positively mark out a candidate.

- 'First-time' writers who are college-based might profitably seek out collaborative possibilities with colleagues or trainers who have already published in relevant academic journals.

- Collaborative work with more immediate colleagues is probably especially desirable, bringing with it the potential to enhance the collegial ethos of an institution.

- The personal satisfaction of seeing one's work in print – and perhaps even on sale – is great.

- A further, linked, source of satisfaction lies in being involved with the dissemination of best practice to fellow mentors and others.

- When writing about matters such as the professional development of trainees, ethical issues need to be accorded special importance. This applies with special force to the area of trainee underperformance, when inadvertently allowing individuals to be identified could be viewed very seriously – not just ethically but legally.

- There are frustrations often in store because of the time-lag between submission of work to a journal and its eventual publication. Commonly, journal articles will be reviewed by two independent referees before an intention to publish can be confirmed. Editorial and technical processes can add further delays – to the extent that a piece of writing can seem (to its author(s) more than its readers, sometimes) to be quite dated by the time it appears.

- A strategy to avoid such slightly frustrating experiences might be to seek internal opportunities to publish (e.g. in college newsletters/bulletins) and/or journals which are unrefereed.

- 'One thing might lead to another', as published work can stimulate the interest of academics, editors and other parties reading it and this can bring about approaches to further develop ideas, or to write on related themes – to end this list of points on a positive note.

Some 'horizon-scanning'

As I observed in introducing this guide, mentors are now at the very centre of current thinking with regard to initial teacher education. Further consolidation of their role, and refinement of their approaches, will in my view be witnessed over the coming years. I would anticipate that seeking a formal qualification could become far more of a majority pursuit amongst mentors – especially as almost certainly more universities and organisations will follow the lead of institutions such as Oxford Brookes University and the Chartered Institute of Personnel and Development in offering attractive routes to accreditation. Furthermore, we may increasingly find colleges placing successful mentoring far more prominently in their criteria for the award of 'advanced skills' status. As the observation of classroom teaching becomes an even more important dimension of various quality systems, so there will be an expanded requirement for *observer training* and mentors will surely have much to offer here.

At present there is an emerging tendency on the part of government (if not, for obvious reasons, on the part of universities involved in ITE) to promote an even greater devolution of core training functions to employers/placements, and such a scenario would have notable implications for the need to expand the mentoring 'pool'. Already in the schools sector mentors have a stronger, formalised, involvement in judging trainees' eligibility for the award of their qualification to teach. Amongst some politicians and even educationists there is a lingering sentiment that schemes such as 'SCITT' (School-Centred Initial Teacher Training) offered the best – or at any rate least contaminated by 'barmy theory' – approach to preparing new entrants for the realities of classroom life. (The use of 'training' as opposed to 'education' in the designation of the schemes probably spoke volumes for their objectives.) Should such views come to hold sway then the confidence and readiness of mentors to assume even greater responsibilities, within a significantly wider jurisdiction, will be all-important. So too will be the capacity of mentors to exercise their professional judgement even at the stage of selecting trainees with the potential to become effective teachers; a number of HEIs are in fact already involving practising mentors in this function, acknowledging the high value of their inputs to the process.

But the skills of mentoring are supremely transferable ones, to reiterate this key point yet again, and merely being involved in such an activity as, say, training others who will need to conduct a large number of teaching observations by no means sets a limit to the developmental opportunities which may be taken advantage of. Alongside this kind of role – and the intrinsic satisfactions and rewards of mentoring that were summed up in Chapter 5 – there are other avenues to explore. Ever-widening participation in post-compulsory education is likely to trigger the development of more all-encompassing *student mentoring* schemes, and there will be a job to be done in contributing to the design of these. *Peer mentoring*, in particular where a key objective is the support and retention of specific cultural groups which the profession needs, will need strengthening. 'Even managers need mentors' and there are opportunities for mentors who also have – or will go on to have – management experience. On the other hand, for mentors opting, for whatever reason, to scale down their commitment to full-time PCET-based employment there are very often, it seems, ways open to acquire consultancy work in coaching and/or mentoring. More broadly, much training and development work, both within and outside of the post-compulsory sector, will far more confidently be approached with a background in mentoring. While it would be to wildly overstate the case to say something like 'only be a mentor and anything's possible', the possibilities touched on here surely are not exhaustive.

Not everyone will find that they are drawn to mentoring as a professional activity, and not everyone will wish to continue with it on a long-term basis. It would be dishonest not to acknowledge that for some college-based practitioners the appeal of other endeavours – pastoral work with students, say, curriculum management, or acquiring important responsibilities for resourcing and developing elearning – will hold greater appeal. But for those choosing to further exploit the attributes and skills that led to their initial involvement in mentoring, I would say that these are exciting times.

References

CEL (2004) *Mentoring: Learning from Practice, Learning from Each Other*, London: Centre for Excellence in Leadership.

Cohen, L., Manion, L., and Morrison, M. (2000) *Research Methods in Education* (5th edn), London: RoutledgeFalmer.

Derrick, J. (2004) Developing mentoring skills, *Professional Development (Basic Skills Bulletin)*, 1 (October).

FENTO/AoC (2001) *Mentoring towards Excellence,* London: Further Education National Training Organisation/Association of Colleges.

Guest, G. (2004) No longer an optional extra, *Adults Learning* 16/3 (November): 22–4.

Appendix 1
Relevant journals

As in all academic fields, there has been a proliferation of journals over recent years. Many are available in both printed and electronic form, while some are only produced as electronic sources for internet access. Those listed below are mostly available in both formats; some are generally UK-focused, others have a far more international flavour. Even those journals in section (A), below, will from time to time carry articles in which mentoring features; clearly those in section (B) have a more specialist focus.

(A)

Journal of Education and Work
Journal of Further and Higher Education
Research in Post-Compulsory Education
Teacher Development
Journal of Vocational Education and Training

(B)

International Journal of Mentoring and Coaching
International Journal of Evidence-Based Coaching and Mentoring
Mentoring and Tutoring: Partnership in Learning

Appendix 2
A selection of useful websites

The caution here is an obvious one: websites come and go. While some in the following list are relatively well-established, and do not appear 'at risk', others may emerge as being of little more permanence than the 'pop-up shops' we have started to see. The websites of governmental and non-governmental bodies may well, in the present turbulent times, be at risk of name changes – or ceasing to exist altogether.

www.aoc.co.uk – Association of Colleges: offers a management perspective on the sector's challenges and successes

www.basic-skills.co.uk – Basic Skills Agency: focuses specifically on the important area of adult basic skills

www.bbc.co.uk/learning/ – The BBC's major learning and teaching site: although not a website that is in any way PCET-specific, it is invaluable for both for its links to other educational websites and for ideas in the areas of resources and activities.

http://www.bis.gov.uk/fe – Department for Business, Innovation and Skills (BIS): the government department that at the time of writing oversees policy for the colleges.

www.city-and-guilds.co.uk – City and Guilds: a greatly respected source of guidance on the huge range of vocational qualifications offered by this board.

http://education.guardian.co.uk – *Guardian* Education: includes a separate section dealing with further education that is often of great interest.

www.lsis.org – Learning and Skills Improvement Service: showcases various examples of innovative practice in the sector, and makes available its publications.

www.niace.org.uk – National Institute of Adult Continuing Education: an excellent site both covering policy issues and illustrating best practice in the education of adults.

www.ofsted.gov.uk – Office for Standards in Education: for practitioners, probably the best reason to access this site is to read inspection reports of other PCET institutions, to gain a sense of what the inspectorate is judging to be (in)effective practice in learning and teaching in the sector.

www.tlrp.org – The Teaching and Learning Research Programme: although the projects funded under the auspices of the TLRP are now concluded, for the present at least the important project summaries and reports of some highly significant work carried out in PCET remain accessible here.

Appendix 3
Assignment briefing

What is critical incident analysis?

Critical incident analysis is a useful tool for reflecting on teaching and professional practice more generally. It is the identification of 'critical incidents' from your own professional experience. A critical incident may be a commonplace, everyday event or interaction, but it is 'critical' in that it stands out for you. Perhaps it was problematic, confusing, a great success, a terrible failure, or captures the essence of what you are trying to achieve in teaching and learning.

Critical incidents are considered as major turning points in professional life, but they may not always be discerned as such instantaneously. Their nature and significance may only become evident following a process of reflection and/or discussion with others.

Analysing critical incidents

1. Choose a critical episode: this would be something that stands out for you, e.g. a successful or unsuccessful teaching/learning incident, a problem presented to you by students (communication difficulties, low attendance, etc.).
2. Describe the incident to include:
    - when and where it happened (time of day, location and social context);
    - what actually happened (who said or did what) – what you were thinking and feeling at the time and just after the incident.

3. Interrogate your description to include:
   - why did this incident stand out?
   - what was going on?
   - were there different levels of 'behaviour' or activity?
   - did I bring personal bias or a particular mindset to the event?
   - could I have interpreted this event differently from another point of view?
   - what can I learn from this episode?
   - what can I do to progress a resolution of the problem/s it suggests?
4. Find a friend or colleague to:
   - share your account of the episode;
   - discuss your interpretation;
   - modify your analysis, where necessary, in the light of peer suggestion, advice, perspective.
5. Where appropriate, you may want to compare your analysis with the views of other key people involved in the episode (students, colleagues, etc.).
6. Write up your report – the detail you chose to include depends on the purpose of the report. If you name colleagues and students, clarify issues of confidentiality.

References

Cunningham, B. (2008) Critical incidents in professional life and learning, in B. Cunningham (ed.), *Exploring Professionalism,* London: Bedford Way Papers, Institute of Education, University of London, pp. 161–89.

Gray, D., Griffin, C., and Nasta, T. (2005) *Training to Teach in Further and Adult Education* (2nd edn), Cheltenham: Nelson Thornes.

Hillier, Y. (2005) *Reflective Teaching in Further and Adult Education* (2nd edn), London: Continuum.

Hoyle, E. (1995) *Professional Knowledge and Professional Practice,* London: Cassell.

Tripp, D. (1993) *Critical Incidents in Teaching,* London: Routledge.

Wenger, E. (1998) *Communities of Practice: Learning, Meaning and Identity,* Cambridge: Cambridge University Press.

Notes

Introduction

1 The title of this qualification is an interesting and significant illustration of the increasing currency of 'Learning and Skills' as a description of what in this book I will continue to refer to as the post-compulsory education and training (PCET) sector. So too, of course, are the designations of what have become the two principal stages in the process of achieving QTLS: introductory certification is in the form of PTTLS – Preparing to Teach in the Lifelong Learning Sector – and subsequently the DTLLS is worked towards, the Diploma in Teaching in the Lifelong Learning Sector.

2 Standards prescribed by SVUK were brought into operation in 2007; they are unlikely to survive beyond 2011.

3 NEETS: 'Not in education, employment or training'.

4 Note, for instance, the Doctorate in Coaching and Mentoring (DCam) now being offered by Oxford Brookes University.

1 Mentoring in context

1 In this book I will generally use the term 'trainee' to describe those beginning teachers that mentors are supporting, largely because doing so aligns with OfSTED terminology. However, in the literature of mentoring readers will encounter such alternatives as 'protégé', and 'mentee', the former being especially prevalent in connection with mentoring in business and commercial environments. At least one UK teacher training provider describes its trainees as 'interns'. One other point to make is that employed teachers following in-service programmes would not necessarily recognise themselves as trainees, and may well reject the term, especially if they have in fact taught for some time.

2 The post-compulsory sector itself is increasingly being described in official documents as a Learning and Skills sector (LSS). Indeed, as referred to in my Introduction, official recognition of being properly qualified to teach in the sector is bestowed by holding 'QTLS'. However, it is observable that a wider constituency, seemingly including the majority of college teachers themselves, as well as many training providers, continue to use PCET, as an abbreviation for post-compulsory education and training. Some readers may feel that the use of 'FE' should have been opted for in the book, if we recall the simple

contention of the seminal report 'Learning Works' that 'further education is everything that does not happen in schools or universities' (Kennedy, 1997: 1).

3   A total of 17 objectives were listed.

4   See also Cunningham (2008).

3   Mentors and models of professional learning

1   In this particular case, senior college managers who have themselves elected to be mentored.

4   Observing classroom teaching

1   Certificate in the Teaching of English to Adults.

5   The rewards and challenges of mentoring

1   This has now become part of a new PCET institution, 'K College'.

2   Ainley and Allen forcefully illustrated these aspects of PCET's post-incorporation tribulations ('market-managed consolidation'): 'while student numbers spiralled to over four million today, the number of colleges in England fell from 465 to 373 with the loss of more than 20,000 staff' (Ainley and Allen, 2009: 10).

6   Working with other colleagues in problem-focused contexts

1   To frame matters rather differently, the term *solution-focused* is of course available to us: however I am choosing to make absolutely explicit the fact that from long experience I recognise it is the incidence of *problems* that tends to trigger a need for collaborative approaches, hence the title of the chapter.

Index